DECORATIVE

Mini Murals

you can paint

KERRY TROUT

NORTH LIGHT BOOKS

CINCINNATI, OHIO
www.artistsnetwork.com

Other fine North Light Books are available from your local bookstore or art supply store, or direct from the publisher.

06 05 04 03 02   5 4 3 2 1

Library of Congress Cataloging-in-Publication Data

Trout, Kerry.
    Decorative mini-murals you can paint / Kerry Trout
        p. cm.
    Includes index.
    ISBN 1-58180-145-9 (alk.paper)
    1. House painting—Amateurs' manuals. 2. Mural painting and decoration—Technique. 3. Interior decoration—Amateurs' manuals. I. Title.

TT323.T76 2002
745.7'23—dc21   2001054607

Editor: Gina Rath
Production Coordinator: Kristen D. Heller
Designer: Joanna Detz
Layout Artist: Kathy Gardner
Photographers: Christine Polomsky and Al Parrish

ABOUT THE AUTHOR

Kerry Trout has been painting and drawing since childhood. Aside from commercial art courses in college, she is completely self-taught. She has become known locally for her unique designs on painted furniture. Kerry works out of her storefront studio in central Indiana where she does custom work and holds weekly painting classes. She is the author of two other North Light books: *Handpainting Your Furniture* and *From Flea Market to Fabulous*. She lives with her husband, Tom, and her constant companion, an 11-year old dachshund named Heidi.

You may write to her at:
Studio on The Square
West Marion Street
Danville, IN 46122

You can also see more of her work at:
www.kerrytrout.com

Metric Conversion Chart

TO CONVERT	TO	MULTIPLY BY
Inches	Centimeters	2.54
Centimeters	Inches	0.4
Feet	Centimeters	30.5
Centimeters	Feet	0.03
Yards	Meters	0.9
Meters	Yards	1.1
Sq. Inches	Sq. Centimeters	6.45
Sq. Centimeters	Sq. Inches	0.16
Sq. Feet	Sq. Meters	0.09
Sq. Meters	Sq. Feet	10.8
Sq. Yards	Sq. Meters	0.8
Sq. Meters	Sq. Yards	1.2
Pounds	Kilograms	0.45
Kilograms	Pounds	2.2
Ounces	Grams	28.4
Grams	Ounces	0.04

DEDICATION

For my parents

ACKNOWLEDGMENTS

*I'd like to thank the following persons who contributed
in some way to the making of this book:*

Kathy Cook

Bethe Ferguson

Kathy Kipp

Christine Polomsky

Gina Rath

Sharon Spencer

Mr. and Mrs. David Thompson

Meredith Thompson

Tom Trout

Special thanks to:

Genifer Bilker

Patty Bucy

Rosemary Reynolds

Chris Wallace

TABLE OF CONTENTS

INTRODUCTION

Murals on walls have sure become popular. And with good reason. Artists see a blank wall as an empty canvas, and what those artists are doing with those walls is remarkable. Anything from giant Roman pillars or grape vineyards, to frolicking dolphins are transforming rooms. Pick up any home décor magazine and you'll see at least one muraled wall featured. It used to be that muraled walls were only in the formal areas of the home, mainly the foyer and dining room, but now they're everywhere and everyone wants them!

If you have ever painted a mural on a wall, or several walls, you know what a mammoth task it is. If you're working alone, like many of us do, a room-size mural can be arduous and exhausting. And to a new artist, the thought of painting an entire wall might be quite intimidating and overwhelming. Well, that's the reason I wrote this book. I want to show how muraling can be done on smaller surfaces as well as large surfaces. If painting a wall mural is something you really want to try, how about getting your feet wet first with something smaller, like a window shade or a door? I also give you three trompe l'oeil wall projects that are small enough to finish in an afternoon.

Some of the projects in this book are meant to be painted life-size, but all other projects are ones that could be enlarged to life-size, if it's a grander scale you want.

A word about photocopying: There are strict but complex laws that protect copyrights. In a worst-case scenario, the shop owner who makes illegal copies could actually have his copying equipment confiscated. It's no wonder the local printer is leery of making a copy of anything with a copyright © symbol on it. If that's the case, take this book along and have the printer refer to the copyright information at the front of the book.

CHAPTER ONE
Materials

GENERAL SUPPLIES

Make sure you have all the supplies needed for a particular project. Some supplies can be substituted, but please don't ever use a cellulose kitchen sponge in place of a natural sea sponge, or use masking tape in place of painter's tape just because they're less expensive. Masking tape is *not* painter's tape. Using it in place of the required painter's tape can ruin a painting. I'm not sure why it's called masking tape, because I wouldn't use it to mask anything! It's just too tacky and will pull up any previous paint you have applied. Painter's tape may not always be labeled as "painter's tape," but it will say "low-tack" or "safe-release" and will be either purple, blue or snow white. It comes in several widths and is a wonderful aid and a must-have for mural painting.

I also suggest you wear appropriate clothing or a painting apron. Acrylics are water-based, yes, but also permanent. I'll always remember the look of horror on a student's face when, after she had gotten paint all over her sweater and jeans, exclaimed, "You mean this doesn't wash out?!"

BRUSHES

Use the best brushes that you can afford and have a wide array of sizes on hand. The way your painting turns out is almost solely determined by the condition of the bristles in your brush. Use new flat brushes for floating. As difficult as it is to learn to float colors, you will have an even tougher time if you try to use a worn-out flat shader. When your flat brushes begin to show wear and no longer hold a sharp chisel edge, demote them to base coaters. The same goes for the rounds: If they don't bounce back to a sharp point and hairs begin to splay, add them to your line of scruffies.

Rinse your brushes thoroughly and often, and clean them well after each day's use. Lay them on a paper towel to dry. I always lay the handles of the wet brush on top of the handle of another brush. The brushes are then drying at a slight angle and any water left in the ferrule will flow out. Stand your brushes bristles-end-up only *after* they are dry. If water is left in the bristles, it can seep down into the ferrule and cause damage.

When using one brush for a long period of time, stop occasionally and clean it with soap and water or brush cleaner. This will remove any paint that has begun to dry near the ferrule.

As you're painting, remember to use each brush for the purpose for which it was designed. Always use the full width of a flat brush. For instance, you should never apply paint with the corner of a flat brush. Take advantage of the design of the brush and use the specific brush that is called for in a project. If you are using a ¼-inch (6mm) shader loaded with Avocado, and the next step calls for a no. 1 round loaded with the same color, change brushes. Don't use the shader where the round is needed just because you have Avocado already loaded.

I always recommend that you use a large water basin. You'll have cleaner water and will need to change it less often.

And never, never allow your brush to stand in water!

PAINTS

I use and recommend DecoArt Americana acrylic paints, and all the projects in this book were painted with that paint. DecoArt has so many colors that many distributors do not have the display space for all of them; so there might be a few colors I use that you can't find. Don't worry, feel free to use the closest color you have. If the directions call for Marigold and all you have is Golden Straw, substituting one yellow for another isn't going to affect the outcome of your painting—as long as the color is extremely close. This goes for most other colors as well.

If you are using a brand of paint other than DecoArt, you need to use your brand's equivalent of the colors I use. *The Decorative Painting Color Match Sourcebook*, by Bobbie Pearcy (Tru-Color Systems, 2000), is the bible of color-matching. Bobbie has done all the mixing and experimenting for you, and her work has now set the industry standards for color matching paint. Tru-Color Systems has also come out with the first computerized color wheel, so now you can match colors with the use of your computer (see Resources, page 142).

Acrylic paint is cheap and goes a long way, but two ounces of anything is not a lot, so don't waste your paint. Squeeze out only what you need. In most cases, what I call "a dime's worth" (a puddle of paint no larger than the size of a dime) is plenty. And in many cases even a pea-size portion of paint is enough. Just use common sense when squeezing it out. Don't scrape back into the bottle what you don't use, as it has had time to set up while out on the palette and actually has started to dry. You don't want to mix this with the fresh paint.

If you have a bottle that's clogged, take the cap off and use a toothpick to clear the hole. Push the clog out of, instead of into, the bottle. Pushing the dried paint into the bottle will only contaminate the fresh paint and clog up your cap again.

When using DecoArt Americana Satins, you must use wax-free transfer paper; otherwise your transferred pattern won't adhere to the painted surface.

The more you paint, the more you'll find out how helpful it is to understand color theory. Every artist should know that red and yellow create orange and that every color in the spectrum is derived from the mixing of the three primary colors: red, blue and yellow. Buy a color wheel. These are helpful guides and available at any fine art supply store.

Feel free to mix colors if you like. I mix paint on my palette all the time when I want to achieve just the right tint or shade of another color. If I need a tint lighter than Jade Green, then I'll add just a touch of white to it. I will also mix colors when I don't have the particular color I need. If I want a certain shade of mauve, I might mix Pansy Lavender, Boysenberry Pink and Slate Grey. And I wouldn't know how much of which color until I saw the perfect shade on my palette. Hint: Never mix more than three colors to achieve a final color.

Liquid Shadow

A mix I use frequently is one I call Kerry's Liquid Shadow. This is an equal mixture of Lamp Black, Burnt Sienna and Prussian Blue (1:1:1). To this mixture add an equal amount of glazing medium (1:1). Store the mixture in an airtight container.

The Liquid Shadow is applied with a dabbing motion, then quickly diffused with a mop brush to eliminate any hard edges. More than one coat can be applied once the previous coat has thoroughly dried.

GENERAL TIPS

Following are a few painting tips that you may find useful in mural painting or any painting you do.

When you feel yourself becoming fatigued or even frustrated, put your brush down and quit for the day. Remember, we are painting for the pure enjoyment of it. You will be rested and have a fresher outlook in the morning.

If painting a project, such as the Trompe L'oeil Cat, on the wall over a door or window, position your ladder or scaffold so that the artwork is eye-level. This will ensure accurate artwork and will also be the most comfortable for you.

As I remind you in the book, acrylic paintings are done working from the background of the scene to the foreground.

Don't cut corners. There is a reason for every step I have taken while painting the projects.

Don't get ahead of the instructions. Example: A project shows a cluster of leaves. If the instructions tell you to paint the background leaves only, then do so, but don't paint the foreground leaves. There's a reason why you don't want to paint them just yet. In most cases I will explain why you do something only part way. And not only will I tell you to do something, but I will tell you why it is done.

One more important thing I want to mention is: when the directions say to "allow the first coat to dry thoroughly"—let it. The paint may look dry, but if it feels cold when touched with the back of your finger, it's not dry. Applying a second coat to a layer of paint that is not dry can cause an "ulcer." This is when your brushstrokes start picking up and removing the first layer of paint. Have patience. And finally, relax, enjoy, and have fun. Isn't that the whole point?

CHAPTER TWO

Techniques

Unless you're a seasoned decorative painter, there may be a few terms or techniques in this book you are unfamiliar with. The techniques take only a minute to learn, but longer to master; and the only way to do that, and feel comfortable with applying them, is to practice. Mastering these techniques will greatly improve your skills as a painter and give you the confidence to take on more advanced projects.

I use just about every technique listed here in all of my projects. Using them is how I achieve depth, contour, realism, shading, uniformity and any other detail important in my painting. If you are like many new painters who compare their projects to the one in the picture and say "What did I do wrong?" it's most likely because you haven't mastered the techniques that the artist used. Practice these techniques until you have them down pat. And when you do, you will approach a project with eagerness and confidence, and not with the "I don't know how this is going to turn out" attitude. You will know how it's going to turn out because you will have the skills you need to make all your projects turn out great!

FLOATING

Floating is a term used often in decorative painting instructions. It is one of the most difficult techniques to master, probably because it is so unforgiving. Either you do it right or you don't. And this is why my students dread it! But rest assured you can learn it and do it well. And this is one of those techniques that has to be followed to a T or it won't come out right. The industry has recognized this problem, and there are a few mediums on the market now that aid in floating colors. I recommend DecoArt's Easy Float. This is a silky-feeling clear medium that is added to water. Loading your brush with the treated water helps the color flow effortlessly from the bristles. I also like to use an extender on the surface before I float. Extender is a medium that keeps the paint from drying too fast. It extends the open time—the time you have to manipulate the paint before it gets tacky. (I use DecoArt's Brush 'n Blend extender.)

Floating is a technique you need to practice until you become adept and comfortable with it. But if you follow the directions on the next page, you'll soon master it.

FLOATING

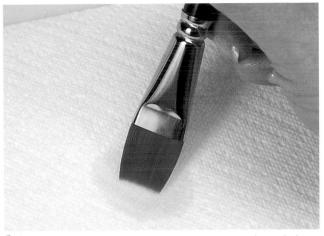

1   Brush a very thin layer of extender along the area you will be floating on. Put one ounce of water into a small cup and add one drop of Easy Float. Use this water for loading only—not for rinsing your brush. Use the largest flat brush you have when floating. Dip the bristles into the float water and bring it up soppy wet.

2   Lightly touch the bristles to a paper towel until the "shine" is gone from the bristles. The brush should still be plenty wet. This is a good time to mention excess water above the bristles. After rinsing your brush, take care to remove those pesky drops of water that stick to the ferrule. If allowed to remain, they will drip down the bristles just as you are making a stroke.

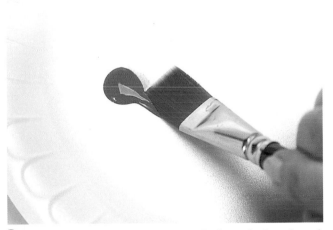

3   Drag just the corner of the brush through the edge of the paint. This should be very fluid paint and fresh from the bottle.

4   Wipe the brush back and forth flatly against one spot on your palette and watch it carefully. You will see the paint begin to float across the bristles. When this happens, it's ready to be applied to your surface. Place the paint end of the brush against the edge you want to float on and pull your stroke across the surface, using the entire width of the brush. Make sure your brush is perpendicular to the object you are floating around. For example, if you are floating around the outside of a circle, the chisel end of your brush will always be lined up to the center of the circle, as a hand would sweep around a clock.

DAMP BLENDING

This is a technique that I use constantly. It's one that could probably be replaced with floating, but for me there are times to float and times to damp blend. This technique is also a lot easier than floating. When the directions say to damp blend, it means to use a clean, damp (not wet) brush.

Let me explain what actually happens in this technique. When you put paint in your brush and apply it to the surface, the paint flows out of the bristles. Quickly rinse the brush and wipe the excess water out; then when you put the brush back down on the paint, you'll notice the brush now acts as a wick and begins to take paint off the surface. When you damp blend, you wipe with your brush and "wick" away the paint on only one side of the stroke to create a soft edge.

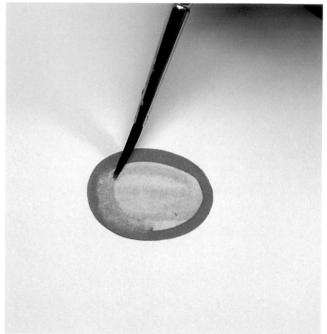

1 Here I have painted a circle, but I want to damp blend the edges. Actually I need to diffuse the inside edge of that paint stroke, to soften it.

2 Rinse the brush, and gently sweep back over the still-wet paint, but on the inside only.

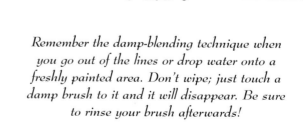

Remember the damp-blending technique when you go out of the lines or drop water onto a freshly painted area. Don't wipe; just touch a damp brush to it and it will disappear. Be sure to rinse your brush afterwards!

MAKING A WASH

When asked to make a wash of a color, you need to add a lot of water to the paint so it is transparent and almost colorless. Here I have made a wash of Deep Periwinkle. See how much it is diluted? A wash should be applied with a flat wash (or shader) brush or a mop brush. A wash will take longer to dry than paint because it is mostly water. Don't apply a wash to a vertical surface—you'll have a drippy mess.

DRYBRUSHING

Drybrushing is a great way to show texture in wood and tree bark. It's also useful when you want just a hint of opaque color. I have seen various definitions of dry-brushing. When I instruct you to drybrush, I mean for you to use the following procedure: Load a *damp* brush (usually a flat) with paint; then wipe the paint back off on a paper towel. When the brushstroke is skippy and rough-looking, then it's ready to apply to the surface. Drag the bristles across the surface and "dry" streaks of paint will be the result.

COMMA STROKES

Everyone should master comma strokes. They are the most used, versatile stroke in decorative painting. The Zhostovo-style painting requires a lot of comma strokes, as does the single-stroke art popularized by the early Bavarian artists. Peter Hunt, a pioneer in decorative furniture painting, could do a stylized couple in Victorian dress, surrounded with birds and flowers, all done with nothing but comma strokes.

Comma strokes can be straight, shaped like a tear drop, or curved, like the punctuation mark. They can be made short and squat using a round brush or long and elegant using a script liner. No matter what shape or size, they are basically stroked the same way.

1 The first rule is to properly load your brush. When using a round brush, load the brush generously up to the ferrule. Hold the brush at an angle and press it against the surface until the bristles begin to fan out.

2 Begin to pull your brush toward the hand that is holding the brush. As you pull the brush, arch it slightly. Here I have made an exaggerated arch so you can see it well. As you begin to make that arch, begin lifting so that the stroke becomes thinner. The end of the stroke should have a thin sharp tail.

PULLED PETALS

Here is a quick and easy way to make flowers. Load your brush (here I am using a medium round) generously and make comma strokes, beginning on the outside edge of the flower petal and stroking in toward the center of the flower. Curve the strokes just slightly to make the petal look natural.

DOUBLE LOADING

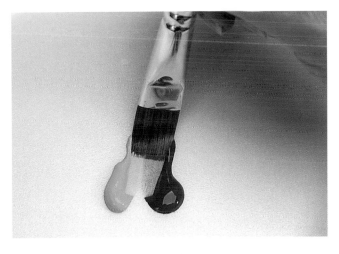

To double load a brush, dispense two colors onto the palette close together. Run the flat side of the brush down the middle so that each edge of the brush picks up color. As you did for floating, wipe the brush back and forth on your palette. Repeat until the colors meet each other in the middle of the bristles. Then you are ready to apply the paint to the surface.

PULLED LEAF STROKE

Pulled leaves are very easy to do and are good to use when you have a lot of leaves to paint. You can also vary the look of the leaves (as nature does) by inverting, or changing colors. To make a pulled leaf, hold your double-loaded brush at an angle; press down while pulling at the same time. As you pull, slowly turn the brush so that the leaf ends in a point. Practice this stroke and you will see how many different shapes you can make and still get them to look like leaves. Angling the brush severely and pulling it out will give the appearance of a leaf that is facing another direction. Be sure to make the pulled leaves different widths. When you look at a tree, all the leaves aren't facing flat toward you. They are going in every direction.

WHAT'S A "TOUCH"?

Often I make a color by adding "just a touch" of another color to achieve a desired tint or shade. You may ask, "How much is a touch?" The truth is there is no one answer because it depends on how much paint you are using. Sometimes I might add a touch of white to a quart of pink to get a slightly lighter pink. On a smaller scale, I might add a touch of black to a little puddle of white to get a light gray. It really depends on what color you need to achieve, not the amount you need to add. In these projects, we are mixing colors right on the palette, so if I want to achieve a deep teal, I'll add just a touch of yellow to blue, as pictured. The amount may be more or less, but just know that it is a very small amount compared to what I am adding "the touch" to.

16

STIPPLING

I use stippling primarily for trees. It's so forgiving it's fun! The brush does all the work, and you can enjoy creating foliage that seems to appear before your eyes. The key is the brush. Use a scruffy brush. A scruffy is an old, battered paint brush with misshapen bristles. Don't throw away an old round brush that won't perform anymore—demote it to a scruffy. The deerfoot stippler is a brush that is designed just for stippling, but I have not found one yet that works as well as my "real" scruffy.

1 Dampen your scruffy brush and wipe dry. Dip it into full strength paint (here I've used Avocado); then blot it off on a paper towel. Pounce the brush up and down on the surface and it will make irregular blotches of color. For distant trees, do less pouncing around the outside to leave a soft edge.

2 To highlight the foliage, there is no need to rinse the brush—just dip it into a lighter color (here it is Jade Green) and pounce it onto one side of the first layer. (Pay attention to your light source.) Pounce the color into the darker color, slightly blending the two.

THINNING PAINT

One of the most common questions my students ask when thinning paint is, "how thin is thin?" This is very important when you are using the rake brush or the script liners. The paint must be thin for these brushes to perform properly. This usually means it's about half water and half paint and should be translucent on the palette.

If you have a deerfoot stippler that won't stipple, load it with Snow-Tex, or any similar gritty-textured snow medium. Let it stand in the brush overnight to dry. Then wash it out with brush cleaner. Your stippler should be scruffier and work much better.

USING YOUR RAKE BRUSH

The rake brush, sometimes called the comb, is a specialty brush that is designed to make very fine hair and grasses. It accomplishes this because the ends of the bristles do not come to a sharp flat edge but are thin and staggered. There are enough bristles in the body of the brush to hold the paint, yet the paint flows onto the surface from very fine individual end hairs that are longer than all the others. This is how we are able to simulate hair and fur easily. Paint has to be extremely thin to flow from these fine hairs in order to get the desired look. In fact, the rake brush is so delicate that it simply won't perform if the paint is too thick. To make hair or fur, load the brush then hold the brush perpendicular to the surface and pull down with short, quick strokes, lifting to a taper as you end the stroke. Make grass by simply flicking the strokes upward.

USING YOUR LINER BRUSH

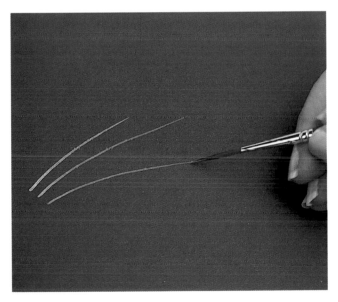

Learning to use the liner brush well is the key to perfect animal whiskers. The liner brush requires a very thin consistency of paint. The paint must flow fluidly to achieve fine lines, and whiskers are just about as fine as you're going to get. If the paint is too thick, the brush will skip and you won't paint a convincing whisker.

If you apply the paint too thickly, the whiskers will look like twigs. So practice making those thin lines, and always remember "Thin Brush, Thin Paint."

Load your liner well with paint thinned to an inky consistency. Make sure the bristles are massaged to a sharp point. Hold the brush close to the ferrule and place just the tip on the surface. Quickly brush outward in one smooth sweep while curving the stroke slightly. Begin lifting until the stroke ends in a tapered point. Once you put the whisker down, it's down, and there's not much chance of correcting it. Practice on paper until you feel comfortable enough to paint whiskers on the surface. They are almost always the last thing you'll paint on the animal.

Bunny Triptych

These little guys are among my favorite subjects to paint. Bunny murals are fun in kitchens, children's rooms, sunrooms or wherever you choose. Wouldn't they be cute on a potting shed or patio wall or sitting on a sunny window sill? Here I've painted two contented little bunnies among the garden tools on a small triptych. You could give this as a unique gift or just place it on your desk for your own enjoyment.

MATERIALS

BRUSHES 18/0 liner, 2/0 script liner, no. 1 round, no. 3 round, ¼-inch (6mm) filbert rake or flat rake, ¼-inch (6mm) flat, no. 8 flat, no. 10 flat, no. 20 flat, small and large scruffy brushes **ADDITIONAL SUPPLIES** small sea sponge, white transfer paper, latex gloves, Scotch tape, DecoArt multipurpose sealer, DuraClear Satin Varnish **SURFACE** hinged wooden triptych from Walnut Hollow

PAINTS = DecoArt Americana; Dazzling Metallics (DM)

Jade Green	Light Buttermilk	DeLane's Deep Shadow	Titanium White

Heritage Brick	Mistletoe	Avocado	Black Forest Green

Kerry's Liquid Shadow	Slate Grey	Sterling Silver (DM)	Ebony Black

Honey Brown	Milk Chocolate	Bittersweet Chocolate	Sable Brown

Venetian Gold (DM)	True Ochre

PATTERN

These patterns may be hand-traced or photocopied for personal use only. Enlarge the pattern above at 167% and the pattern at right at 143% to bring them up to full size.

The dotted lines above represent the outline of the wooden triptych.

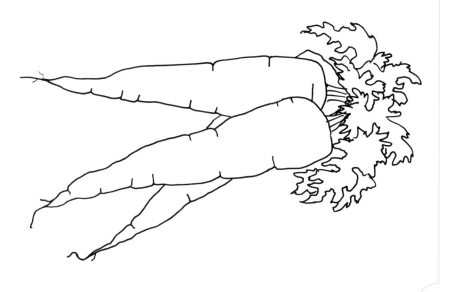

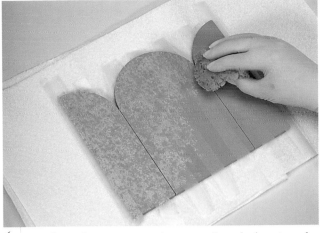

1 | Apply multipurpose sealer over the whole triptych including the hinges. Using your small sea sponge, basecoat the front, back and edges of the piece with Jade Green.

Once dry, use Scotch tape and tape stripes about ¾-inch (19mm) apart across the center outside panel. Mix Jade Green with a touch of Light Buttermilk to lighten. Tap your small dampened sea sponge into the paint; then dab onto the surface to paint the stripes. Make these stripes as light as you want. I chose to make mine very subtle. Carefully pull off the tape.

2 | Turn the triptych over and trace the pattern on the inside using white transfer paper. When you come to the seed packet, transfer only the basic outline at this time.

Remember, in acrylic painting, you begin painting the background and move forward; so start with the flower pots in this project. Basecoat the terra-cotta pots with DeLane's Deep Shadow using your no. 8 flat. Mix DeLane's Deep Shadow and Titanium White (2:1) and drybrush onto the center of the pots.

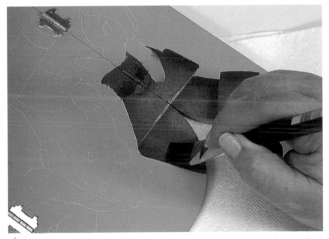

3 | Add just a bit more Titanium White to this mixture and drybrush this on top of what you just drybrushed, not extending over the edges.

With that same color on the chisel edge of your brush, paint along the top edge of both flower pots. Toward the center of the flower pot rim use straight Titanium White on the chisel edge of the brush.

4 | Using your no. 20 flat, float Heritage Brick along the edges and underneath the rims of each flower pot.

You may want to use your hairdryer
to speed the drying time.

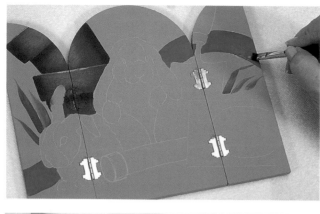

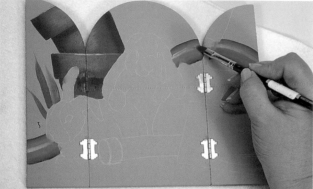

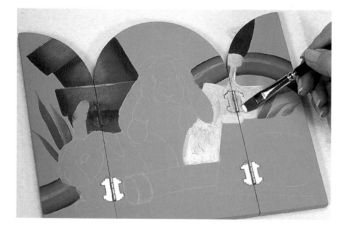

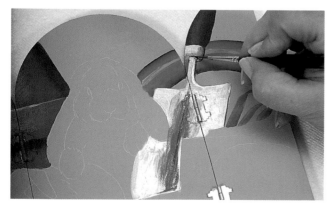

5 | With your no. 8 flat and Avocado, pull through on the chisel edge to make a few blades of grass on the outside edges of the triptych.

Working from back to front and using your no. 8 flat, basecoat the background portions of the hose with Mistletoe (exclude the front part of the hose for now). Dry thoroughly.

6 | Add just a little bit of Titanium White to the Mistletoe and with the chisel edge of your no. 20 flat, paint down the middle of the hose. Rinse the brush; then damp blend the edges a bit into the darker green.

With your no. 8 flat, float Black Forest Green along the bottom edge of the hose. Float a little on the top also. Using the same brush, float a watery highlight of Light Buttermilk along the upper curve of the hose.

7 | Again using your no. 8 flat, basecoat the trowel with Slate Grey including the ferrule of the trowel. Two coats may be needed. Basecoat the trowel handle with Heritage Brick. Paint over the Slate Grey with two coats of Dazzling Metallic Sterling Silver. Dry thoroughly between coats.

8 | Mix just a little Black Forest Green into Heritage Brick and float this along the right side of the handle. Add a touch of Titanium White to Heritage Brick and with your no. 10 flat, highlight the handle of the trowel.

Mix Ebony Black with Slate Grey to get a dark gray and drybrush this down the center of the trowel. With a little watery Ebony Black add a straight line down the center using the chisel edge of your brush. Use your ¼-inch (6mm) flat with the dark gray mix and float shading on the right side of the ferrule. Shade with Ebony Black where the handle goes into the ferrule.

Drybrush just a little Titanium White highlight onto the neck of the trowel using the chisel edge of your ¼-inch (6mm) flat.

Use the dark gray mixture to shade the neck and the right side of the trowel using your 2/0 script liner.

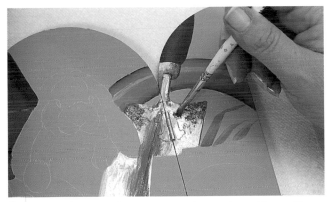

9 Make the trowel appear rusty by applying Burnt Sienna with your no. 3 round to the edge of the trowel; then work in to the center slightly. Use your small scruffy to stipple more rust onto the shovel.

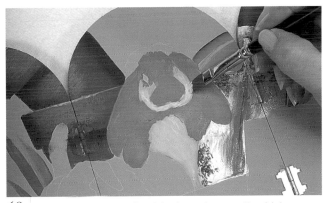

10 With your no. 10 flat, block in the top (back) bunny with Honey Brown and a mixture of Honey Brown and Light Buttermilk (1:1) as shown. You will probably need two coats of each. You can paint around the pattern lines.

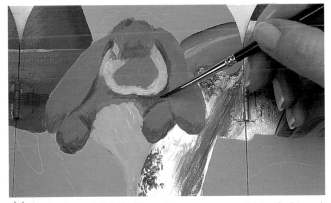

11 Shade with Milk Chocolate using your ¼-inch (6mm) flat. Apply this deep shading around the ears and under the chin with short scruffy strokes. Use your no. 3 round and add deeper shadows with Bittersweet Chocolate.

12 With the ¼-inch (6mm) filbert rake brush (or flat rake), mix Light Buttermilk and Honey Brown (1:1) thinned. Start at the bottom tip of the ear and work upward making small strokes.

13 Where the patches of Honey Brown and the Light Buttermilk and Honey Brown mixture meet, soften with your rake brush and thinned Honey Brown. Do this by overlapping the strokes so the two colors blend. Add Honey Brown to the top of his head as well.

The key to using a rake brush is to use the thinnest paint possible, and reload often.

LOP-EARED BUNNY, *continued*

14 Still using your rake brush but with thinned Light Buttermilk, add tiny hairs around the muzzle and cheek area. Also add these light hairs to the chest area and between the ears on top of the head.

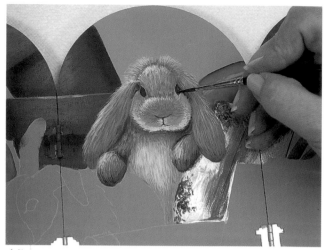

15 With the rake, add Titanium White to the chest, forehead and muzzle. With Bittersweet Chocolate and the rake brush, extend some of the paw hairs over the trowel. Use your 2/0 script liner with Bittersweet Chocolate to define the bunny's toes, the nose and the mouth lines. Fill in the eyes with your no. 3 round and Bittersweet Chocolate.

16 With your no. 3 round, apply a little bit of Light Buttermilk and Honey Brown mixture under the eyes and a little bit over the eyes. Use the same mixture under the nose and to the left side of the nose. Use your 2/0 liner and Bittersweet Chocolate to pull out just a couple of short lashes. Shade the light side of the nose just a bit; then damp blend this in. With the same brush, add the highlights in the eye with Titanium White. Add just a little bit of thinned Honey Brown to the right side of his nose.

DUTCH BUNNY

17 Mix Titanium White and Slate Grey (3:1) for a very light gray color and base in the light areas of the Dutch bunny with your no. 8 flat. Base in the dark areas with Bittersweet Chocolate. While this is drying, go on to painting the ground.

18 Basecoat the ground with Ebony Black, using the largest flat brush you are comfortable with. Use your no. 3 round for smaller areas like under the hose and bunnies. While that's still wet, quickly add Bittersweet Chocolate to the Ebony Black and just blend them together loosely with your ¼-inch (6mm) flat. Add a little Sable Brown and Slate Grey also and with a wet brush loosely blend these colors together back and forth. You still want to be able to see each individual color after they are put down.

Remember, we are working from the back of the picture to the front. Now that you have painted the ground, everything you paint after this will be in front of or on top of the ground.

20 Mix Sable Brown and Bittersweet Chocolate (1:1) and stroke hair all over the dark areas.

19 Add a second coat of Slate Grey to the bunny's body using your no. 10 flat. When you get to the bottom of the bunny's feet, tap some of the Slate Grey over the ground to make the edges of the feet look furry. Shade the dark fur with Ebony Black using your rake brush. Pull little hairs around the edges of the dark areas that are overlapping other areas (but only if the hair is growing that way). Make the hair on the ears a lot finer.

21 Use Sable Brown to add highlights in the dark areas. Pay close attention to the hair growth direction as shown in this photo, and follow it as you paint the fur.

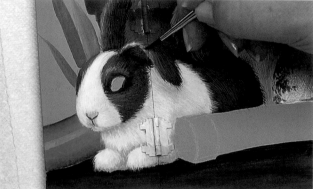

22 Still using your rake brush, stroke deep shadows in the white areas with thinned Slate Grey. Add shadows between the paws, under the chin and under the ear. With Titanium White on your rake brush, paint white hairs over the line where the white shoulder area meets the black area. The two colors of fur are merging and you don't want a straight line there.

23 Use DeLane's Deep Shadow with your scruffy brush to barely tap color into the inner part of the floppy ear. With a 2:1 mixture of Titanium White and DeLane's Deep Shadow, paint in the nose area with your no. 3 round. Shade this with a 1:1 mixture of the same two colors. For the deepest creases of the nose, use a mixture of Bittersweet Chocolate and DeLane's Deep Shadow (1:1). Use Titanium White with your rake brush to highlight from the nose upward to the top of the fore-head, the front of the paws, around the mouth area, the muzzle and a little behind the ear. Use your no. 3 round and a bit of Titanium White to define the lower lip with little strokes. Add highlight hairs near the eye and a few at the front of the ears that face the light.

24 Paint the eyelids with a medium brown mixture of Sable Brown and Bittersweet Chocolate using your no. 1 round. Highlight with a few strokes of DeLane's Deep Shadow and Titanium White (the pink nose color). Paint the inside of the eye with Ebony Black; add a dot of Tita-nium White highlight and a small Sable Brown comma stroke for the iris.

As shown in step 25, use a bit of Honey Brown with your rake brush to pull a few hairs from the paw of the rear bunny onto the back of the Dutch bunny. Add an eyelash or two on his right eye even though you can't see the eye.

25 Paint the rest of the hose just as you did the first part (see steps 5 and 6). Basecoat the brass coupling with two coats of Milk Chocolate using your ¼-inch (6mm) flat. Use your no. 3 round with Bittersweet Chocolate to define the coupling end. Refer to the pattern to see the line. Dip into the Bittersweet Chocolate and flatten the point of your brush a little to paint the inside of the coupling. Leave the small portion uncovered as shown. Because of the angle of the hose, the opening in the end should be oval. Be careful to retain that shape.

26 With your no. 3 round, add the inside threads with Ebony Black and the outside threads using Bittersweet Chocolate. Shade on the bottom of the coupling with Bittersweet Chocolate.

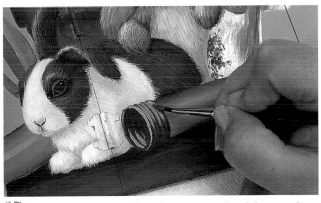

27 Add Venetian Gold to the area inside of the coupling using your no. 3 round brush. Use the same brush and color to follow the threads of the coupling.

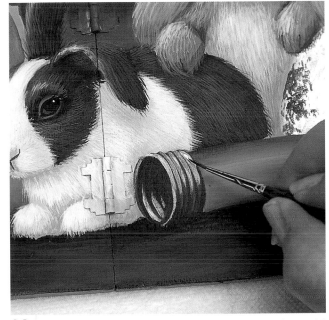

28 Use Titanium White and your 18/0 liner brush to add highlights to the edge of the threads.

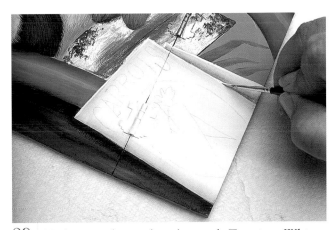

29 Undercoat the seed packet with Titanium White using your no. 20 flat. Then paint the same area with Light Buttermilk. Once dry, trace on the seed packet pattern. Use your no. 10 flat and float Milk Chocolate against the back seed packet. Also shade along the outer edges of the front packet with a more watery float. Outline the upper and left side of the packets with your 18/0 liner and Titanium White.

30 Use Light Avocado thinned slightly on your 18/0 liner and paint in the letters. Hold your brush close to the ferrule for more control with detail.

31 With a watery mix of Honey Brown, outline the oval using your 18/0 liner. Mix Light Avocado and just enough Bittersweet Chocolate to make a deep olive green. Use a very small scruffy brush to pounce on this first color for the leaves.

32 Mix Avocado with a tad of Light Buttermilk to get a light green. Pounce this onto the leaves with the scruffy. With your ¼-inch (6mm) flat, basecoat the carrots with DeLane's Deep Shadow. With the same color add a stem or two to connect the leaves to the carrots. You will need two coats of this light green color.

With Heritage Brick, shade the undersides of the carrots using your no. 3 round. Damp blend this into the carrot colors. Add a float of Milk Chocolate around the carrots. With a mixture of Light Buttermilk and just a touch of DeLane's Deep Shadow, drybrush a highlight using your ¼-inch (6mm) flat.

33 Paint cast shadows in the appropriate places with Liquid Shadow on your ¼-inch (6mm) flat. This will add definition to the bunny and other objects. After the first coat of Liquid Shadow completely dries, add a bit more to the bottom of the hose in front and under the bunny's feet. You can add this anywhere you want deeper shadows.

Load your 18/0 liner with thinned Titanium White and massage the brush in the paint until it comes to a really sharp point. Dip and pull the brush to do this; don't twist it. Paint the whiskers by applying just the tip of the brush at an angle, pulling out lightly and swiftly and applying less pressure as you reach the tip. Pull the brush tip up so it leaves a smooth, fine tapered point. Whiskers come out from the muzzle and arch downward slightly.

34 Use your no. 3 round and Bittersweet Chocolate with a touch of Titanium White to make a charcoal gray color. Also mix Bittersweet Chocolate with a touch of Milk Chocolate to make a lighter brown. Dab these in a horizontal kind of way to create pebbles. Touch in Ebony Black under each pebble for shadow. Add a touch of Bittersweet Chocolate and Titanium White to the top left side of each pebble for highlights. For even lighter highlights add a bit more Light Buttermilk to the last mixture.

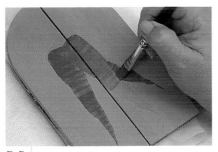

35 | After the inside is completely dry, close the triptych and transfer the carrot pattern to the front two panels. Undercoat the carrots with up to two coats of True Ochre. Dry thoroughly.

With your no. 10 flat, basecoat the carrots horizontally across the carrot with DeLane's Deep Shadow. Use the full flat edge of the flat brush to get the desired horizontal streaks.

36 | Still using your no. 10 flat, dry-brush a highlight on with a mix of Light Buttermilk, DeLane's Deep Shadow and just a touch of True Ochre to achieve a pale orange. Apply this straight down the middle of the carrots.

Shade both sides of each carrot with a float of Heritage Brick. This will not only shade, but will smooth out irregular edges made by your cross-stroking.

37 | Add little wrinkles with your 2/0 liner and a mix of Heritage Brick with DeLane's Deep Shadow.

With a mixture of Titanium White and DeLane's Deep Shadow, highlight the bottom edges of the wrinkles you just added. Continue this highlight down to the end of the carrot.

38 | Paint the stems from the carrots with the dark green mixture (from step 31) and more stems in front of these with the light green mixture (from step 32). Now pounce in these leaves with a large scruffy brush, painting the dark leaves first, then the light using a mix slightly lighter than that used in step 32.

Float Milk Chocolate around the outside edges of the carrots. Add Liquid Shadow to deepen the shadows.

39 | When the paint is completely dry, apply a protective finish with Dura-Clear Satin Varnish.

Trompe L'oeil Window Shade

I think painting a window shade is just plain fun! And if you have a shade that is almost always pulled down, like in a bathroom or in a window with an ugly view, you can change the shade into an unexpected focal point! Shades are so inexpensive that you could even change them for each season.

MATERIALS

BRUSHES no. 1 script liner, no. 2 liner, no. 0 round, no. 3 round, no. 8 flat, ¼-inch (6mm) flat, ½-inch (12mm) flat, 1-inch (25mm) flat, 1½-inch (38mm) bristle or foam **ADDITIONAL SUPPLIES** 2-inch (5cm) blue painter's tape, 1-inch (2.5cm) blue painter's tape, medium-size sea sponge, transfer paper, water-based polyurethane spray **SURFACE** 26-inch (66cm) wide white window roller shade (room-darkening type)

PAINTS = DecoArt Americana; Hot Shots (HS); Satins (S)

Olive Green	Titanium White	Payne's Grey	Avocado
Milk Chocolate	Dark Pine	Black Green	True Ochre
French Grey Blue	Calico Red	Cadmium Yellow	Desert Sand

Deep Burgundy	Crimson Tide	Light Buttermilk	Fiery Red (HS)

Scorching Yellow (HS)	Country Green (S)	Sage Green (S)	Buttercream (S)
Powder Blue (S)	Bright Blue (S)		

PATTERN

These patterns may be hand-traced or
photocopied for personal use only. Enlarge
the corner leaves and the flowers at 143%
and the hummingbird at 125% to bring them
up to full size.

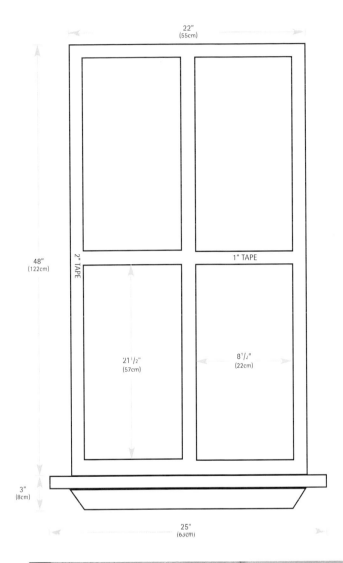

22"
(55cm)

48"
(122cm)

2" TAPE

1" TAPE

21¹/₂"
(57cm)

8¹/₂"
(22cm)

3"
(8cm)

25"
(63cm)

Window Measurements

When beginning this project, decide how wide and how long you want your trompe l'oeil window to be; then center the window onto the roller shade. My window measurements are shown at left.

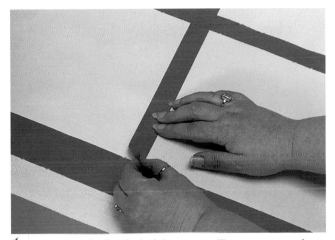

1 You may find it helpful to use a T-square to make sure that your corners are completely square (you want to be very careful your window is not crooked). Then with a pencil lightly mark off the outside measurements of the window. Apply 2-inch (5cm) blue painter's tape to the inside of the markings. This will mask off the frame of the window. Decide where you want the mullions (the sections of wood between the window panes) and use 1-inch (2.5cm) blue painter's tape to mask out them out. *Do not use masking tape!*

2 Paint the window panes with Powder Blue and a touch of Bright Blue using your 1½-inch (38mm) bristle brush. Begin at the very top with a scrubbing slip-slap motion to create a somewhat mottled effect. The blue should be darker at the top and gradate to a lighter Powder Blue at the bottom by adding just a touch more White as you move down the pane. Continue with the Powder Blue down to the bottom of the windowpane. Let dry. Before applying the colors, you may want to practice mixing them in order to achieve the desired results.

DISTANT FOLIAGE

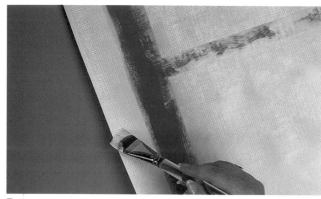

3 Use a 1½-inch (38mm) bristle or foam brush to paint outside of the frame to simulate the wall color. I used Buttercream here, but you could try matching your own wall color if you wish.

4 With a medium-size sea sponge, apply the distant background foliage using Sage Green at the top of the foliage area.

5 Gradate to a darker green toward the bottom by gradually adding Country Green to the Sage Green.

6 Using your 1½-inch (38mm) bristle, brush on Country Green below the sponged area.

7 Wipe the excess paint off your brush and blend the Country Green into the color above. With your 1½-inch (38mm) bristle brush, carry Country Green to the bottom of the pane. Let dry thoroughly and apply a second coat.

8 Block in Black Green at the bottom of both window-panes using your 1-inch (25mm) flat shader. Paint an area about 3 inches (7.6cm) high with an irregular, abstract edge at the top. This will act as deep shading under the leaves, and the abstract edge will help it blend into the foliage. When dry, transfer the leaf pattern onto the window shade.

9 Block in the geranium leaves with Avocado using your ½-inch (12mm) flat shader.

10 Thin Olive Green and use your ½-inch (12mm) flat shader to sweep the color from the outside of the leaf inward. Turn the brush to end your stroke with a taper. Do this on each side of the leaf. Dry thoroughly.

11 Drybrush Olive Green onto the edges of the leaf (on top of what you have already applied) and taper off toward the middle. Use a thin mix of Avocado and Black Green (1:1) and your no. 2 liner to stroke on veins. Start with the center vein and then do the outer veins. When painting side veins, always start your stroke at the center vein and stroke outward toward the edge of the leaf, lifting your brush slightly to end your stroke with a thin line. Shade the stem with this same color, but only near the top of the leaf where it would naturally be shaded.

12 Sparingly apply Scorching Yellow with your ¼-inch (6mm) flat shader to the outermost edges where the Olive Green was applied. This will intensify and highlight the green. Thin Olive Green and use your no. 2 liner to go over the veins you already painted. This helps give a bit of dimension to the veins.

13 The leaves at the top of the window shade are made with two pulled-leaf strokes. One half of the leaf is done at a time. Here I used Americana Satins Country Green, Hunter Green, and Sage Green. Paint darker leaves around the edge of the window and lighter ones toward the center. Draw a pencil mark to indicate the center vein of the leaf you are going to paint. Load your ½-inch (12mm) flat with color. With the brush perpendicular to the surface, put one corner of the the chisel edge of the brush down at the top of the pencil line and at a 45° angle from the line. Pull toward the other end of the line and press down at the same time. Keep the edge of the chisel that is on the line straight, and do not allow it to flare out too much—it may help to pivot the brush slightly. End the stroke on the chisel edge again, making a thin tapered point to the leaf. Repeat for the other half of the leaf.

GERANIUMS

14 | Using your no. 8 flat, add pulled petals for the geraniums with two coats of Crimson Tide. Paint four petals in each cluster.

15 | Add more petals to the left side of each cluster with Calico Red.

16 | Tip the top of the petals with Titanium White using your no. 3 round. Once the white dries, paint over the Titanium White with Fiery Red. This will go on pink but will dry to a vibrant red.

17   Transfer on the pattern of the hummingbird. Under-coat the hummingbird with Titanium White using your no. 8 flat.

18   Shade the back and the back of the head with Dark Pine plus a touch of Titanium White using your no. 3 round.

19   Still using your no. 3 round, apply an additional layer of Titanium White to the belly area. Add a touch more Titanium White to the Dark Pine to make it a little lighter than the green on the hummingbird's back. Paint short strokes of this mixture in between the green and white. Blend slightly.

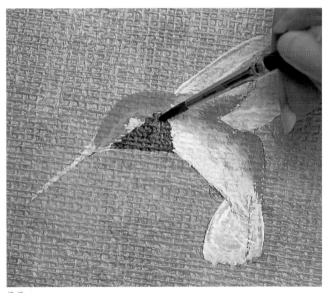

20   Using your no. 3 round, add Titanium White with a touch of Deep Burgundy to the underbelly area. Also paint in the throat with Deep Burgundy plus a touch of Payne's Grey.

21 Paint the wings using your ¼-inch flat with French Grey Blue and a touch of Titanium White.

Detail and shade the tail with Payne's Grey using your no. 2 liner. Detail and shade the wings with Payne's Grey using your no. 3 round and no. 2 liner for the fine lines.

22 Highlight the wings and tail with diluted Titanium White using your no. 3 round and no. 2 liner. Highlight the throat with Deep Burgundy with a touch of Titanium White using your no. 3 round. Pick up a touch more Titanium White and add a highlight under the eye.

23 Outline the upper part of the body with Black Green using your no. 3 round. Damp blend inward to diffuse the brushstroke. Shade the belly with a watery mix of French Grey Blue and then blend it into the Titanium White. Outline the underside of the bird with Payne's Grey using your no. 1 script liner. Damp blend into the belly area. Shade around the ruby throat and the eye with dabs of Payne's Grey using your no. 3 round.

24 Paint the eye, beak and feet with Payne's Grey using your no. 0 round. Highlight the beak, eye and feet with a mix of Titanium White and Payne's Grey using your no. 3 round. Using your no. 1 script liner, paint a few dabs of Titanium White above the eye and shoulder of the wing. Dab a speck of Calico Red on the throat using your no. 3 round to "slightly brighten" the hummingbird's ruby throat.

25 Remove the tape and basecoat the mullions with Light Buttermilk. Allow to dry; then mark off ¼-inch (0.6cm) margins on each side. Allow the lines to form corners in the center.

26 Using your ½-inch flat shader, paint the shaded sides with Desert Sand. Pay attention to the light source. The light source is coming from the upper right side.

27 Still using the same brush, paint the highlighted edges on the tops and left sides with Titanium White.

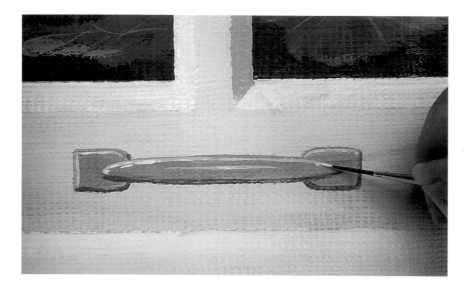

28 | Allow to dry completely. For the handle pattern, trace the image at left and adjust the size to fit your blind. Basecoat with True Ochre using your ¼-inch (6mm) flat and shade with Milk Chocolate using your no. 1 liner. With the same liner, highlight with Cadmium Yellow and add a reflective light with Titanium White.

29 | Add a shadow to the handle with Desert Sand and your no. 8 flat.

30 | Mask off the sides of the window ½ inch (1.2cm) beyond the frame. Apply a shadow around the window with a mix of Buttercream + Milk Chocolate + Payne's Grey (8:3:1) using your 1-inch (25mm) flat. Darken the mix with more Milk Chocolate and run a line close to the frame using your no. 1 liner. Remove tape.

31 Remember that flat acrylic paint comes to life after it is coated with polyurethane or varnish. For this project I would recommend spraying your shade with a water-based polyurethane. Both poly and acrylic paints are very pliable, so rolling and unrolling the shade will not harm the artwork. However, be sure the final coat is completely dry before rolling up the shade.

Schoolhouse Notebook

Here is a unique way to brighten up and personalize a notebook for that special teacher. For this project I wanted an authentic one-room schoolhouse to paint, so I went to a historic colonial village and photographed one. What teacher wouldn't be delighted to receive a beautiful gift such as this? You can also personalize the notebook for that added touch. Don't be surprised to see your project displayed at the front of the teacher's classroom.

MATERIALS

BRUSHES 2/0 script liner, 8/0 liner, 18/0 liner, no. 2 liner, no. 2 round, no. 3 round, no. 8 flat, no. 10 flat, no. 12 flat, no. 20 flat, ¼-inch (6mm) flat, ⅜-inch (10mm) mop, ¼ inch (6mm) mop, ½-inch (12mm) comb, small scruffy **ADDITIONAL SUPPLIES** white transfer paper, multi-purpose sealer, DuraClear Satin Varnish, painter's tape **SURFACE** 3-ring binder (vinyl cover) from any school supply or variety store

PAINTS = DecoArt Americana; Dazzling Metallics (DM)

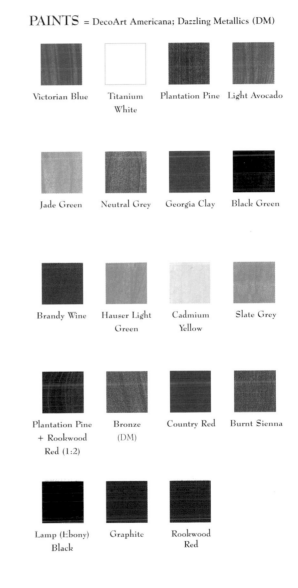

Victorian Blue | Titanium White | Plantation Pine | Light Avocado

Jade Green | Neutral Grey | Georgia Clay | Black Green

Brandy Wine | Hauser Light Green | Cadmium Yellow | Slate Grey

Plantation Pine + Rookwood Red (1:2) | Bronze (DM) | Country Red | Burnt Sienna

Lamp (Ebony) Black | Graphite | Rookwood Red

Pattern

These patterns may be hand-traced or photocopied for personal use only. Enlarge the pattern above at 175% and the pattern below at 200% to bring them up to full size.

Mrs. Miss Ms. Mr.

Aa Bb Cc Dd Ee Ff Gg

Hh Ii Jj Kk Ll Mm Nn

Oo Pp Qq Rr Ss Tt

Uu Vv Ww x Yy Zz

1 | Seal the surface with multi-purpose sealer and under-coat with Neutral Grey. With your no. 20 shader, paint the grass beginning with Jade Green at the top of the horizon line and gradating down to Plantation Pine.

Paint the sky in the same way, using Victorian Blue at the top and gradating down to the horizon by adding Titanium White. The colors don't have to meet at the horizon line since it'll be covered by trees. Allow to dry thoroughly; then trace on the pattern.

2 | With Black Green on your no. 20 shader, lay down the deepest shadow in the most distant foliage just above the grass line. Use an upward stroke so you create an irregular tree line.

3 | Use painter's tape to tape off the edges of the school-house. Mix Black Green and Plantation Pine and use your ⅜-inch (10mm) mop to pounce on foliage half the way up the trees. Pounce in a forward motion so the bris-tles in front of the brush leave a ragged edge. Switch to Plantation Pine only and continue pouncing the foliage.

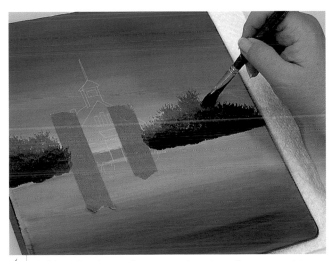

4 | Add Light Avocado to your brush and pounce this onto the top of the tree line in the same manner.

5 | With your ¼-inch (6mm) mop brush, pounce Hauser Light Green on just the tips of the branches. This is almost a dry-brush application. Pounce on the upper right branches of each section of trees, just the very tips. Be sure to cover the pattern lines.

TREES, *continued*

6 | Still using your mop brush, drybrush Cadmium Yellow onto the upper right side of the Hauser Light Green. Then come down into the darker foliage and tap in a few areas to designate a few shorter branches.

7 | Mix Georgia Clay with a tiny bit of Cadmium Yellow to make a yellow-orange color. Highlight the trees just slightly with this yellow-orange using your ¼-inch (6mm) mop.

Add a bit more Georgia Clay so you have a little deeper orange; then highlight just the tips of the trees.

SHRUBBERY, FENCE AND GRASS

8 | Still using the mop brush, pounce in some Light Avocado shrubbery against the dark shading. Highlight these in the same way as you did the trees. This will soften any dark lines.

9 | On the left side (shaded side) of the school, paint the picket fence Slate Grey using your 2/0 script liner. Paint the fence Titanium White on the right side (sunny side) of the school.

With Jade Green on your ½-inch (12mm) comb, add the most distant grass on the right side and cover the very bottom portion of the fence. Do the same on the left side with Light Avocado.

10 Carefully remove the tape and basecoat the front of the schoolhouse with Brandy Wine using your no. 8 flat and your no. 3 round. Mix Rookwood Red with Plantation Pine (2:1) to paint the shaded side of the schoolhouse. You will need two coats (allow to dry thoroughly between coats). Use your 2/0 script liner to shade the window frames, the louvers in the belfry and the door frame.

11 Using your no. 3 round and Graphite, paint the left side of the roof. Wiggle your brush to make the shingles visible on the back end of the roof.

With the same brush, paint the overhang and the edge of the shingles on the right side of the roof with Slate Grey.

12 Using your ¼-inch flat, add a little Slate Grey to Graphite and paint the front of the belfry roof and the little roof over the door (overhang). Use just straight Lamp Black to shade the underneath side of the belfry roof. Also make a few horizontal marks to suggest shingles on the main roof, the belfry roof and the overhang. Shade the bottom edge of the main roof and add a few little lines on the belfry roof. Highlight the front edge of the belfry roof using Slate Grey with a touch of Titanium White.

Also paint in the shingles on the belfry roof, the front edges of the main roof and the overhang with the same brush and the Slate Grey and Titanium White mixture.

13 Shade in the transom above the door with Lamp Black using your no. 3 round with a nice sharp point. Fill in the windows the same way. I always find it better to outline the window first, then fill it in.

14 Mix Brandy Wine with Cadmium Yellow (1:1), and use your 2/0 script liner to highlight the window frames, the louvered window in the belfry, and the windowsills. Also highlight around the door frame and on the front underneath edge (fascia) of the roof line.

SCHOOLHOUSE, *continued*

15 Use Rookwood Red and your no. 3 round to shade under the eaves. Also paint the shadow of the overhang and the left fascia. Add a touch of Lamp Black to this dark shade and run this underneath the overhang to create the shadow. Use what's left on the brush to paint the braces on the overhang.

Switch to your 2/0 script liner and with this same color make a deeper shadow under the right eave. Go back to the Cadmium Yellow and Brandy Wine mixture (step 14) to highlight the right edge of the braces.

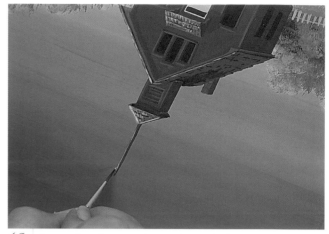

16 Paint the chimney located on the backside of the roof with Burnt Sienna using your no. 2 round. Add just a touch of Lamp Black to Burnt Sienna to paint in the left side of the chimney. Add a second coat to that side.

Turn your work upside down and with Burnt Sienna and the same brush, paint the spire from the base to the tip with one stroke. Shade the spire using your 2/0 script liner and a bit of Lamp Black. Highlight with Titanium White and a touch of Burnt Sienna.

WINDOW PANES

17 If you need to, reposition the pattern onto your notebook to add windowpanes, or lightly sketch them in with a pencil. Starting with the three top windows, line in all the front windows with Slate Grey on your no. 2 liner. First, paint a very thin line going down the center (mullion); then add the horizontals.

For the windows on the shaded side of the school, add a little Lamp Black to the Slate Grey and paint only the left side of the windows as the right side wouldn't be visible from this angle.

18 With the same brush add in the left side and bottom of the front window frames using Titanium White. Add white highlights on the left side of each mullion since they're just partially being hit by sunlight. Thin Slate Grey with water and use your 8/0 liner to make a few diagonal strokes across the windows to suggest reflection.

Use your no. 8 flat and Titanium White to paint the door.

19 With your no. 2 round and Slate Grey, shade the top of the door where the shadow of the overhang is cast. Note: Because the door is recessed, the shadow on the door will be lower than the rest of the overhang shadow that is cast on the front schoolhouse wall. Also run a line of Slate Grey down the right side of the door.

Switch to your 18/0 liner and paint in the door panels with very fine lines of Slate Grey. Add a tiny comma stroke for the door handle.

20 Add shading around the foundation of the school-house with Black Green and your ¼-inch (6mm) flat. With Plantation Pine mixed with a little Black Green, add the longer shadow using the chisel edge of the same brush. Add the cast shadow on the right side of the little tree (you will paint the tree in step 26) at the same time.

21 Use your small scruffy brush to pounce in the lower half of the shrubs with Black Green. Next pounce in Light Avocado and follow this with Hauser Light Green. For the highlight on the bushes, add a little bit of Titanium White to the Hauser Light Green. These are painted the same way as the background trees.

Paint the steps with Burnt Sienna on your no. 2 round.

22 Add a little Titanium White to the Burnt Sienna and with the same brush, paint a line for the highlight on top of each step.

With the same brush and a thin mix of Plantation Pine and Rookwood Red (1:2), paint a shadow on the front wall to the left behind each clump of bushes.

PATH, FLAGPOLE AND APPLE TREE

23 | Mix Jade Green and Titanium White (2:1) and with your no. 10 flat lightly add some highlights in the grass. This helps to cover any pattern lines that may show through; it also gives the grass area some interest.

With the same brush, take a thin wash of Burnt Sienna and squiggle out a path from the steps into the yard. You can streak in some Titanium White to vary the tones in the path.

24 | Load your 2/0 script liner with thinned Slate Grey and paint the flagpole by starting at the top and slowly pulling down. Using the same brush, run Titanium White along the right side of the pole. With Burnt Sienna on the same brush, dip-dot a brass ball onto the top of the pole. After it dries, highlight the right side of the ball with Titanium White.

With your 2/0 script liner, basecoat the lower part of the flag with Titanium White. Mix Victorian Blue with a spot of Lamp Black to achieve a navy blue color, then paint the upper part of the flag.

25 | Still using your 2/0 script liner, paint two or three Titanium White dots on the blue to make stars. Using Country Red and the same brush, add a few red stripes to the flag.

With Graphite and the 2/0 script liner, add the tree trunk and branches. Shade them slightly on the left side with a little bit of Lamp Black. Highlight on the right side with Titanium White and a touch of Slate Grey.

Mix Burnt Sienna and Cadmium Yellow (1:2) and with your scruffy brush, pounce in the foliage base. Add a little more Cadmium Yellow to the mixture and pounce this in on the right side. Finally, pounce in solid Cadmium Yellow to the right side of the foliage.

With each paint mixture, touch in a few little fallen leaves on the ground. Add just a line of Plantation Pine underneath each leaf to give some shadow to the ground.

26 | Add the stair railings with Slate Grey on your 2/0 script liner. Highlight with Titanium White.

Use your no. 2 liner with Graphite to paint in the branches of the apple tree. Shade these with a touch of Lamp Black mixed with the Graphite.

With Hauser Light Green on your no. 10 flat, add little pulled leaves (see page 15) along the bottom of the arch. Having the lighter leaves at the bottom gives the appearance of sun shining through the foliage.

27 Using the same brush, pick up Light Avocado and paint the leaves above the first leaves. As you continue moving upward, use Plantation Pine. Then finally, use Black Green around the outside edges.

28 Use Titanium White and your ¼-inch (6mm) flat to undercoat the apples, placing them wherever you'd like them to be located. Once dried, add Country Red over the Titanium White base.

29 Still using your ¼-inch (6mm) flat, float Rookwood Red in a U shape on the underside of the apple. Drybrush Cadmium Yellow into the unshaded area of the apple.

30 Accent the tops of the apples with Hauser Light Green on your no. 2 round. This is still basically a dry-brush application. With Plantation Pine and the same brush, make a small comma stroke on some of the apples where the stem would be. On the other apples, add a dot for the bottom blossom. Add a thin stem of Black Green from the apple into the leaves.

In every landscape, add a few birds.
They bring life to the painting!

31 Add little comma strokes of highlights to each apple using Titanium White and your no. 2 round. Paint more leaves using Black Green on your no. 10 flat brush, overlapping the apples just a bit with the leaves. Do the same with Plantation Pine.

With thinned Black Green on your 18/0 liner, add a few birds flying in the air by painting a slightly scalloped line.

32 To properly fit the name you want on your notebook, first place tracing paper over the dry notebook, then draw a pencil line across the paper where the name will be placed—this should be at least 1 inch (2.5cm) from the bottom edge. This is your baseline.

Turn to the pattern on page 44 and carefully trace over the letters, one by one, spelling out the name. I recommend black ink for this. Be sure to line up every letter on the baseline. I have provided several titles to help you get started. Unless the name is very long, you will need to enlarge the pattern, so use a copy machine and enlarge the name pattern until it is no wider than 9 inches (22.9cm).

Trim down the enlarged pattern if you want and position it onto the notebook. Make sure it is centered and straight. Use painter's tape to tape on both ends; then slide white transfer paper underneath to transfer the pattern onto the notebook.

Use Black Green to first outline the letters using your no. 2 round. Then switch to your ¼-flat (6mm) to fill in the lettering with the Black Green.

Use your 18/0 liner to apply Bronze outlining to the lettering. When using the liner brush, it helps to hold your hand close to the ferrule and keep the brush almost straight up and down, always pulling toward you.

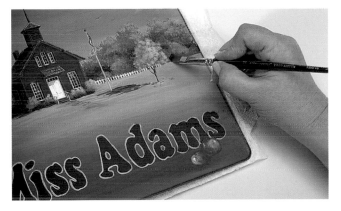

33 | Once the lettering is dry, add two apples to the bottom right-hand corner. Follow the same steps as for the apples on the top of the notebook.

Problem solver: I noticed that the value between the background trees and the tree in the yard was too close. So I used my no. 12 flat and floated some Black Green around the edge of the foreground tree. This helped to separate the two areas and bring the little tree forward.

34 When completely dry, protect the painting on the notebook with DuraClear Satin Varnish.

Goldfinch Frame

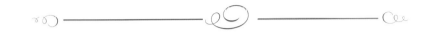

These frames are popular to paint on and they come in all sizes. Although they're meant to be picture frames, I decided to make the frame the artwork itself because anything in the middle might compete or get lost. The simple answer was a mirror!

MATERIALS

BRUSHES Plaid stippler brush 30128, 2-inch (51mm) foam brush, no. 2 script liner, 2/0 liner, 10/0 liner, 18/0 liner, no. 2 round, no. 3 round, no. 6 round, ¼-inch (6mm) flat, no. 8 flat, ½-inch (12mm) flat, ½-inch (12mm) rake, small and medium scruffy **ADDITIONAL SUPPLIES** DecoArt Wood Sealer, white latex primer or gesso, white transfer paper, DuraClear Satin Varnish **SURFACE** Wooden frame from Walnut Hollow, Inc.

PAINTS = DecoArt Americana

Light Buttermilk   Light Avocado   Plantation Pine   Victorian Blue

Avocado   Titanium White   Hauser Light Green   Jade Green

Cadmium Yellow   Summer Lilac   Pansy Lavender   Black Green

Royal Purple   Olde Gold   Salem Blue   Burnt Orange

Lamp (Ebony) Black   Bittersweet Chocolate

PATTERN

This pattern may be hand-traced or
photocopied for personal use only.
Enlarge at 172% to bring it up to full size.

1 Seal the entire surface with wood sealer. Prime with white latex primer or gesso. Basecoat the entire surface using your 2-inch (51mm) foam brush with Light Buttermilk. Practice stippling ahead of time. If you use the same colors when practicing, you will see if you need to adjust the color mixture to achieve the look you want. Mix Victorian Blue with water (1:1) and brush it onto the surface using your sponge brush. Paint, then stipple a section at a time. The paint needs to be wet enough to manipulate with the stippler.

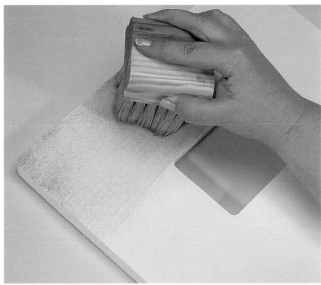

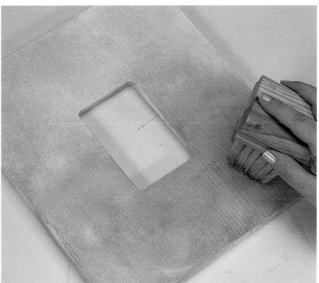

2 Cover the front of the frame with the blue. The blue background should even be behind the green you will be stippling next. Carry the blue over the inside and outside edges also. Adjust the color if needed. You can always add a little Light Buttermilk to the mixture if the blue is too dark. Wipe off the stippler with a dry towel but don't clean it with water until after step 3. A dry brush ensures a thin, even coverage of color. Allow the stippled blue surface to dry completely before proceeding.

3 Mix Light Avocado and water (1:1) and repeat the stippling process over the bottom third of the frame (over the blue). When dry, stipple Plantation Pine (using the same method of application) over the Light Avocado, covering the bottom quarter of the frame (shown in the photo with step 4). This is just the background; it doesn't have to be perfect.

4 | Be sure the surface is completely dry, then transfer the pattern to the surface with gray or white transfer paper. Use whichever you will see best in each area.

With your ¼-inch (6mm) flat, basecoat in the large leaves. Use Plantation Pine and Black Green (2:1) for the foreground leaves, and for the background leaves use Avocado. Use your no. 2 round for tight spaces. You will need two coats of each. Do the same with the smaller leaves, using Avocado for the basecoat.

5 | Paint veins in the leaves using your 2/0 liner. For the smaller lighter leaves use Plantation Pine, for the larger darker leaves use Plantation Pine with a touch of Black Green. The veins should be darker than the base color of the leaf. They are then highlighted using a lighter color. This gives the vein some dimension.

With the same brush and paint, pull out little barbs on the end of each leaf. Highlight the veins and edges of the dark leaves using a mix of Hauser Light Green with a touch of Titanium White. On the lighter leaves add a little more white to the mix for the highlights.

6 | Still using your 2/0 liner, shade the leaves and add the veins. Use Black Green and Plantation Pine for the dark leaves and Plantation Pine and Avocado for the lighter leaves. Go over those to highlight with a mix of Avocado and a touch of Titanium White.

7 Using your ½-inch (12mm) flat, basecoat the thistle blossom with Pansy Lavender. With your no. 8 flat, basecoat the calyx with Light Avocado and let dry; then shade the left side of the calyx with a float of Black Green.

8 With Pansy Lavender, pull out the "fluff" all around the bloom with your rake brush or scruffy. Shade the lower left side with Royal Purple and again pull out the strokes of fluff. Dot the calyx with Hauser Light Green on your no. 2 round to give it a nubby texture.

9 Mix Summer Lilac and Titanium White (1:1). Using your small scruffy, stipple a highlight on the upper right toward the center of the blossom. Highlight the right side of the calyx with a few dots of Hauser Light Green and a touch of Titanium White.

10 With your 10/0 liner and Avocado, pull long, fine spikes out of the blossom. Also with your liner, dot the spikes with Plantation Pine on the shaded side and Jade Green on the right. Pull a few spikes on the calyx, using Avocado on the right side and Plantation Pine on the left.

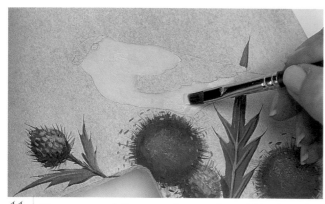

11 Use your no. 8 flat to undercoat the goldfinch with Titanium White. Allow this to dry; then apply two coats of Cadmium Yellow. Make sure the yellow dries between coats.

12 Mix Cadmium Yellow and Titanium White (2:1), and with your no. 8 flat, go over the inside area of the goldfinch, saving the edges. Add just a little more Titanium White to this mix to build the shape of the breast area, the shoulder area and the side of the head. Damp blend this in. Also use this mix to make the white stronger at the base of the tail under the wing.

13 Add a little bit of Titanium White highlights to the shoulder and breast area. Mix Olde Gold and Cadmium Yellow (2:1) and with your no. 8 flat, damp blend this onto the belly and under the wing.

14 With Olde Gold on your no. 3 round, shade the edge of the breast area and damp blend this in. Also shade around the back of the head and on the nape of the neck, the cheek and the scapular feathers.

15 Use your no. 3 round to mix Olde Gold and Black Green (2:1). With this mix, deepen the shading around the lower belly (leg) area and the rump area; then damp blend.

16 | Reinforce the highlighting from step 13 using Titanium White and your no. 3 round. Use very short brushstrokes in the direction that the feathers are growing. Lightly outline the crown of the head and the eye with Lamp Black on your no. 3 round; then fill the areas in.

17 | Mix Titanium White and Lamp Black (1:1) and using your no. 3 round, highlight the crown area with a thin comma stroke. Using your 18/0 liner, outline the eye with this gray mixture. Add just a touch more Titanium White to the same brush and highlight the top and bottom eyelids. With just the tip of your brush add the lightest highlight to the eyeball. These highlights must be very tiny.

18 | Using your no. 3 round, basecoat the beak with Burnt Orange. Add a touch of Lamp Black to the Burnt Orange and paint the separation in the beak; then shade the tip of the beak. Still using your no. 3 round, add a white highlight to the upper and lower beak.

TAIL AND WINGS

19 With your no. 3 round, paint the tail Lamp Black. At the base of the tail use the Olde Gold + Black Green mix (from step 15) to blend the yellow feathers into the black feathers.

20 Mix Lamp Black and Titanium White (1:1) and using your no. 3 round, paint three stripes down the middle of the tail, beginning with the middle stripe. Start at the tip and pull in toward the head. Paint the stripe at the top of the tail thinner than at the bottom because of the angle of the tail.

21 Still using your no. 3 round, add Titanium White to the tip of the tail and around the center feather. Shade the very tip of the tail with the gray mix from step 20.

22 Outline and fill in the wings with Lamp Black on your no. 3 round. If you outline the area first, it's easier to keep the contour and shape of the wings.

23 With your no. 8 flat, float Titanium White to individualize the feathers. Turn the surface so you're pulling the strokes toward you.

24 Using your no. 3 round and a mix of Lamp Black and Titanium White (1:1), add a layer of dark gray feathers.

25 Add just a tinge of Lamp Black to Titanium to make a very light gray. Stroke this mixture onto the tips of the shorter wings with your no. 3 round. Paint a ring of this mix below the shorter wings. In the middle of the back there is a split in the wings; be sure not to cover this up. Add this mix to the front wings as well. With Titanium White on the same brush, whiten the light areas toward the top of the bird and on the front of the wings.

26 If needed, replace the pattern and retrace the legs. Using your no. 3 round, add a little Titanium White to the Burnt Orange and paint the legs and the feet. Make the toes disappear into the blossom of the thistle. With your 2/0 liner, add a tiny bit of Lamp Black to Burnt Orange and paint the base of the legs and the undersides of the legs. Shade the rear leg a bit more since it is behind the other leg.

27 Still using the same brush, add Titanium White to the Burnt Orange for a light peach color; then highlight the feet using little dash strokes. That will bring out the scaliness of the bird's feet. With your no. 3 round, pounce some Royal Purple onto the thistle around the feet and under the belly area. This will create a shadow on the thistle.

Nest

28 Use your ¼-inch (6mm) flat to basecoat the bottom of the nest with Black Green and the upper part with Bittersweet Chocolate. Use the same brush to undercoat the eggs with Titanium White. Mix Bittersweet Chocolate and Titanium White (5:1) and with your no. 2 liner, add the first layer of twigs making random X shapes. Be sure to follow the contour of the nest. Keep the tiny cup-shaped nest small and neat.

29 Add more Titanium White to the Bittersweet Chocolate mixture with a touch of Lamp Black to make a taupe color. Paint a second layer of twigs with your no. 2 liner. Continue to make layer after layer of twigs. Continue lightening the value of each layer by adding more Titanium White. Keep the lightest value twigs toward the top of the nest. Highlight some of the twigs with a few streaks of the lightest taupe just along the upper part of the nest.

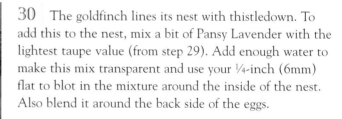

30 The goldfinch lines its nest with thistledown. To add this to the nest, mix a bit of Pansy Lavender with the lightest taupe value (from step 29). Add enough water to make this mix transparent and use your ¼-inch (6mm) flat to blot in the mixture around the inside of the nest. Also blend it around the back side of the eggs.

31 Float a little bit of Lamp Black on your ¼-inch (6mm) flat around the back of the eggs. This will deepen the pocket in the nest.

32 Mix Salem Blue with Titanium White (2:1). Use this and your ¼-inch (6mm) flat brush to basecoat the eggs. Contour the eggs with a fairly wide stroke of Salem Blue on your no. 3 round.

33 Rinse your brush and damp blend the Salem Blue toward the center of the eggs. (See page 12 for damp-blending instructions.)

34 Mix just a bit of Victorian Blue into the Salem Blue and with your no. 3 round, outline the eggs; then damp blend. With the same darker blue mixture, add a few little speckles to the large end of the eggs.

Add one final Titanium White highlight toward the center of each egg.

35 After the paint is dry, use your no. 2 liner and some Bittersweet Chocolate to overlap some twigs in front of the eggs.

Now you need to add the small leaves in front of the nest. Mix Plantation Pine and Black Green (1:1). With this mix and your ¼-inch (6mm) flat brush, add the leaves using the pulled leaf stroke (see page 15). Add stems with your no. 2 liner using Avocado. Shade this with the Plantation Pine and Black Green mixture from step 4.

36 With your no. 2 liner, pull the stems from the main stem to the tip of the leaf with thinned Hauser Light Green. Highlight the leaves with a mix of Pansy Lavender and Avocado (3:1) using your no. 6 chisel blender. Pull the highlight for the upper half of the leaf from the outside in and slant the stroke toward the stem. Inside, start at the vein and stroke out towards the tip.

37 Add some veins in the leaves using your no. 2 liner and Black Green.

38 Mix Cadmium Yellow with a touch of Hauser Light Green and using your 2/0 liner, dot in two or three petals for each of the five-petaled flowers.

39 Mix Cadmium Yellow with a touch of Titanium White and using the same brush, dot in the rest of the petals. Dot the flower middles with Hauser Light Green; then accent with Titanium White and Hauser Light Green (1:1).

40 | When completely dry, protect your frame with DuraClear Satin Varnish.

POSTCARD

THE MOUNT VERNON FROM WEST FRONT

Mount Vernon is owned and maintained by the Mount Vernon Ladies' Association of the Union, founded 1853 for the preservation of the home and tomb of Washington.

Kerry Trout

Covered Bridge Box

In the nineteenth century, it was cheaper to replace a roof than it was to rebuild a bridge. So rural bridges were covered to protect the wooden planks and supports from harsh northern weather.

Living in Indiana, I have been fortunate enough to see and photograph many covered bridges, yet I still stand in awe when I visit one. Covered bridges are one of my favorite subjects to paint, and when I can get away, I like to go out and rediscover them.

MATERIALS

BRUSHES no. 1 script liner, ¼-inch (6mm) flat shader, no. 2 flat shader, no. 4 flat shader no. 8 flat shader, no. 12 flat shader, 1-inch (25mm) flat, no. 0 round, no. 2 round, ¼ inch (6mm) oval mop, small scruffy, ¼-inch (6mm) rake, 1-inch (25mm) foam brush **ADDITIONAL SUPPLIES** DecoArt Wood Sealer, Teflon pad, sandpaper, tack cloth, transfer paper, painter's tape, DecoArt Brush 'n Blend Extender, DuraClear Varnish, clean rag, DecoArt gel stain, straight edge, craft knife, Scotch tape **SURFACE** keepsake box from Walnut Hollow, Inc.

PAINTS = DecoArt Americana; Dazzling Metallics (DM)

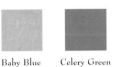
Baby Blue

Celery Green

Black Green

Avocado

Soft Black

Oxblood

Oxblood + Soft
Black (2:1)

Slate Grey

Driftwood

Olive Green

Golden Straw

Burnt Sienna

Glorius Gold
(DM)

Oxblood +
Titanium White
(1:1)

Titanium White

PATTERN

*This pattern may
be hand-traced or
photocopied for
personal use only.
Enlarge at 134%
to bring it up to
full size.*

1 | Lightly sand the surface with a Teflon pad, and remove the dust with a tack cloth.

2 | Seal the top only with wood sealer. Do not seal the sides, as you will be staining them later and wood that has been sealed won't properly absorb stain. After the sealer has dried, lightly sand to remove any raised grain.

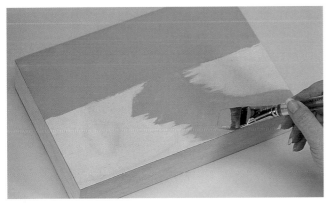

3 | With Baby Blue and your 1-inch (25mm) flat, add the sky and the base for the river. You can "eyeball" the approximate location of the water. Allow the first coat to dry; then add a second coat of Baby Blue.

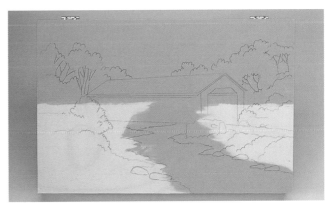

4 | Trace on the pattern, excluding the rocks in the water and the daisies in the foreground. Use a straightedge to transfer the straight lines of the bridge. Touch up the water area if necessary.

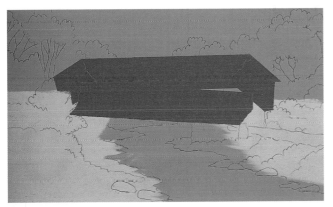

5 | Use painter's tape to mask off the bridge. Trim the tape with a craft knife to get nice clean edges. This will protect the bridge from any paint bleeding on to it from the trees you will stipple behind it.

6 | Stipple in the distant foliage using Celery Green and a small scruffy brush. Make sure you cover the pattern line.

7 Draw in the tree branches using Black Green with a no. 1 script liner. When painting branches, always start your stroke at the trunk and pull the stroke outward, tapering it into a thin line as you lift the brush.

8 Using Black Green on your small scruffy brush, pounce in the deepest shading in the bushes around the bridge and along the bank of the river.

9 Add a touch of Soft Black to Avocado and using the same brush, stipple leaves onto the branches with this darkest shading. These trees appear closer, so they will be darker. Be sure not to add any more color to the distant foliage.

10 Using Avocado, stipple in the middle value shading of the trees as shown.

11 Stroke in additional tree branches using Black Green and your no. 1 script liner. Highlight the trees with a dry brush mix of Titanium White, Avocado and Olive Green using your ¼-inch (6mm) mop. Pounce this highlight mix onto the trees using the drybrush technique on the tip of your ¼-inch (6mm) mop. For the lightest highlight, add a bit more Titanium White to the mixture. Apply the lightest highlights to the upper parts of the foliage only.

12 Paint the grass area under the bridge with Avocado and blend it into Black Green using your ¼-inch (6mm) flat. Remove the tape. Using your no. 1 liner, paint Avocado between the gaps of the roof and wall. Paint the inside of the bridge using Soft Black and your no. 8 flat. Paint the wall studs using Soft Black and your no. 1 liner. Paint the side of the bridge with two coats of Oxblood using your no. 8 flat. Mix Oxblood and Soft Black (2:1) and paint the front end of the bridge using your no. 8 flat. Block in the roof using Slate Grey on the same brush. Using the chisel edge of your brush, run a line of Slate Grey along the right side of the roof.

13 After the surface is dry, tape off the sides of the bridge using painter's tape. Using your ¼-inch (6mm) mop, fill in the background foliage at the end of the bridge with a drybrush mix of Avocado and Black Green.

Using your no. 12 flat, drybrush a mix of Oxblood and Soft Black (2:1) down the outer bridge wall. Occasionally, turn the brush sideways to vary the stroke width.

14 Use a straightedge to pencil in the crossbeams and the windows. Add the cracks and windows to the bridge with Soft Black and your no. 1 script liner.

15 Make some individual boards lighter with a thinned mix of Oxblood and Titanium White using your no. 1 liner. Lighten this mix with more Titanium White and drybrush on brighter highlights to the bridge with your no. 2 round.

BRIDGE, *continued*

16 Basecoat the crossbeam with Oxblood using your no. 2 round. Use the same brush to shade with Soft Black and highlight with Oxblood and Titanium White mixed (1:1). Highlight random boards and the boards under each window with the bridge highlight mix (from step 15) using your no. 1 liner. Do not thin the paint too much. Carefully remove the tape. Paint underneath the eave and the studs using your no. 8 flat and Soft Black mixed with a touch of Oxblood.

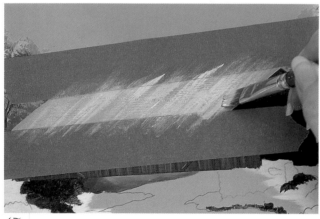

17 Allow the bridge to dry thoroughly; then use painter's tape to tape off the roof area. With your no. 12 flat, dry-brush a mix of Slate Grey and Titanium White onto the roof. Make sure to angle your strokes to follow the pitch of the roof.

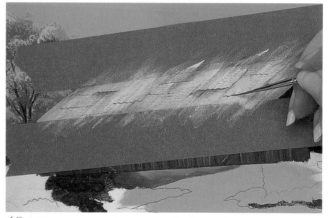

18 Float rust on the roof with thinned Burnt Sienna using your no. 8 flat. Using your no. 1 liner detail the rippled edges of the corrugated tin roof with thinned Slate Grey and a touch of Soft Black.

19 Remove the tape. Using your no. 1 script liner and Soft Black, ripple the overhang edge of the roof. Float Soft Black under the eaves on the front of the bridge using your no. 8 flat. Using the same brush and Soft Black, wash a shadow from the trees onto the roof and also on the side of the bridge.

Create the appearance of weathered wood on the inside of the bridge wall by drybrushing a mix of Slate Grey and Soft Black with your no. 8 flat. Paint the sign with a mix of Slate Grey and a touch of Soft Black using your no. 2 flat.

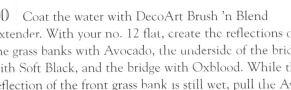

20 | Coat the water with DecoArt Brush 'n Blend Extender. With your no. 12 flat, create the reflections of the grass banks with Avocado, the underside of the bridge with Soft Black, and the bridge with Oxblood. While the reflection of the front grass bank is still wet, pull the Avocado down with the brush.

21 | Basecoat the left bank with two coats of Driftwood using your no. 8 flat. Shade the bank with a touch of Soft Black mixed with a touch of Driftwood. Outline the edge of the bank with Black Green using your no. 1 liner. Using your no. 2 round, dot in the distant rocks with a mix of Titanium White and a touch of Driftwood. Use your no. 2 round to highlight the larger rocks with Titanium White then shade with Slate Grey and a touch of Soft Black. Using your no. 8 flat shader, add the reflections of the rocks in the water with Titanium White.

22 | With Titanium White on your no. 1 liner, paint a thin reflection at the water line of each stone and at the water line of the banks. If necessary, intensify the grass and building reflections. Using the chisel edge of your no. 8 flat, add water ripples with thinned Titanium White.

23 | Basecoat the stone foundation with patches of Slate Grey and Driftwood using your no. 4 flat. With the same brush, paint the road with a mix of Burnt Sienna, Driftwood and Titanium White; also add a touch of Soft Black to the mix to paint the section nearest to the bridge. While the road is still wet, streak in Titanium White and blend slightly. Using your no. 1 liner, outline the foundation stones with a thinned mix of Soft Black and Burnt Sienna. Keep in mind the stones should be irregular in shape.

FOUNDATION AND GRASS

24 Use your no. 1 liner to highlight the top left corner of each stone in the foreground foundation wall with a mixture of Titanium White plus a touch of Driftwood. Highlight the surface bricks with Titanium White and the distant foundation wall stones with Driftwood. Intensify the shading on the foundation wall by outlining random stones with Burnt Sienna and Soft Black.

25 With your no. 2 round, paint the weeds on the far side of the road with Avocado and pounce on some foliage at the base of the entrance of the bridge. Top the weeds on the far right with Avocado plus a touch of Titanium White to make them appear sunlit. Using your ¼-inch (6mm) mop with Avocado, pounce foliage into the remaining unpainted areas on the far bank. Deepen the previous shading if needed by adding Black Green to your dirty brush. Blend the two colors, but do not cover the previous Black Green foliage. Drybrush tufts of highlight on the weeds with a drybrush mix of Avocado, Titanium White and Olive Green using your mop brush. Tip the point of your brush with Titanium White and highlight a few random weeds.

26 Paint some stray weeds at the foundation of the bridge with Avocado and add Titanium White to the Avocado for sunlit weeds. Add sunlit grass to the top of the left bank with Titanium White plus a touch of Olive Green. I use an old rake brush, but you could use any scruffy brush.

27 To achieve the illusion of distance in grass, I always apply the lightest color to the area furthest away and gradate with darker shades to the foreground. Always work from the top down. Begin in the distance with your lightest color and very short strokes (just a pat-pat-pat of the brush). As you work down from the grass at the top, change to Avocado (no need to rinse your brush) make your strokes longer. The closer the grass gets, the longer it appears.

28 Still using your scruffy, continue applying Avocado, then switch to Black Green. Blend the two colors together where they meet.

29 Mix lighter values of Avocado, Olive Green and Titanium White to highlight the tufts of grass using your scruffy.

With the same brush, drybrush Avocado plus Olive Green to make the trees against the end of the bridge. Highlight with Olive Green plus Titanium White using the same scruffy brush.

30 Add the foreground grass with very thin Avocado using your no. 1 liner. Add just a touch of Olive Green to the thinned Avocado and apply the lighter grass. To make long blades of grass, hold the brush straight up and down and gently sweep the brush against the surface, stroking away from you. Apply less pressure at the end of the stroke so that your grass ends in a taper. To make the long grass look natural, angle your strokes randomly, overlap and bend the grasses and make them different lengths and widths. A common mistake is making deliberate strokes when painting grass. Your grass will look stiff and straight if you are too careful, so ease the grip on your brush and make light, swift, haphazard strokes.

31 Using your no. 0 round and Titanium White, paint small comma strokes to form the daisies. Dot the centers with a mix of Golden Straw plus a tad of Burnt Sienna on the same brush. Load the brush with Golden Straw and highlight the centers of the flowers. Make the distant daisies smaller with just one or two petals. Vary the number of petals to create the illusion of the daisies facing in different directions.

At this point step back and look at your painting. I decided to add a few embellishments to mine. I added highlights to the trees, added birds and softened the foliage in a few locations by pouncing in some Avocado. I added more reflective color into the water and deepened the shadows in some spots. I also added splashes of reddish flowers in the grassy areas. Turn to the photo on page 79 to see the effect of these enhancements. You may make these or similar changes or leave the painting as is; it's your time to be creative!

GOLD BORDER

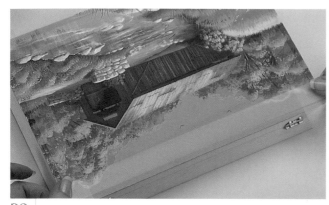

32 | Allow your painting to dry thoroughly. With Scotch tape, tape off a border ¼ inch (0.6cm) in from the edge of the lid. Extend the tape to the corners so the tape will overlap there. Scotch tape is better to use on smaller items when you need a clean line. Because the tape is not textured like painter's tape, the smooth surface will prevent seepage.

33 | With a craft knife, very lightly miter the tape at the corners. Be sure to apply enough pressure to cut through the tape but not through the paint.

34 | Lift one edge of the excess tape and carefully peel it away. Use a smooth object such as a spoon to burnish the outside edges of the tape. Burnishing simply means to carefully rub over the outside edges of the tape (use something smooth and hard such as the back of a spoon) to get a solid seal. This will prevent the paint from seeping underneath, and you will have a good clean line when the tape is removed.

Also measure around the edges ¼ inch down from the top of the lid and tape around the box; then burnish.

35 | Paint the border and the outside edge with the no. 8 flat shader and Glorious Gold. Apply two coats, allowing the first coat to dry thoroughly before applying the second.

36 | When the paint is dry, lift up one corner of the tape with a craft knife, and gently pull it off at a 90° angle.

Varnish the top of the box with DuraClear Varnish. Since acrylic paint is flat, it must be varnished before the antiquing medium is applied to the sides of the box. Once protected, if you get a little on your painting, then it can be easily wiped off. Do not go over the gold with the varnish because this will dull the metallic effect.

37 Mix DecoArt Gel Stain and Burnt Sienna (5:1). Stain the outside edges of the box using your 1-inch (25mm) foam brush.

38 Rub off the stain with an old rag using a light, circular motion. If a deeper shade of stain is desired, you can repeat the staining steps. You can finish the inside of the box as you choose.

39 After the stain is dry, seal with DuraClear Varnish.

Mountain View Lodge

Wouldn't this unique shelf look great in your den or vacation cabin? It's a new piece, but I distressed and antiqued it heavily to create a worn, somewhat masculine look. The painted part of this inexpensive shelf is actually a removable panel. I bought this shelf at a local craft store. The removable insert makes it easier to paint and makes the piece more versatile.

MATERIALS

BRUSHES no. 1 script liner, no. 2 script liner, 5/0 round, no. 1 round, no. 8 flat, ¼-inch (6mm) flat, ½-inch (12mm) flat, 1-inch (25mm) flat, small scruffy, 1-inch (25mm) foam brush **ADDITIONAL SUPPLIES** sandpaper, wood filler, painter's tape, Teflon pad, large rough rock, awl, X-Acto knife, dark brown antiquing wax, wax stick or white candle, palette knife, transfer paper, DecoArt Brush 'n Blend Extender, DecoArt DuraClear Varnish, DecoArt Clear Gel Stain **SURFACE** available at craft stores

PAINTS = DecoArt Americana; Americana Satins (S)

Blue Chiffon	Baby Blue	Titanium White	Country Blue
Olive Green	Avocado	Black Forest Green	Black Green
Driftwood	Golden Straw	Lamp (Ebony) Black	Milk Chocolate
Titanium White + Country Blue (2:1)	Titanium White + Country Blue (1:1)	Olive Green + Avocado (6:1)	Olive Green + Avocado (1:1)
Birch Bark (S)	Milk Chocolate + Ebony Black (1:1)	Ebony Black + Titanium White (1:1)	Titanium White + Driftwood (1:1)

PATTERN

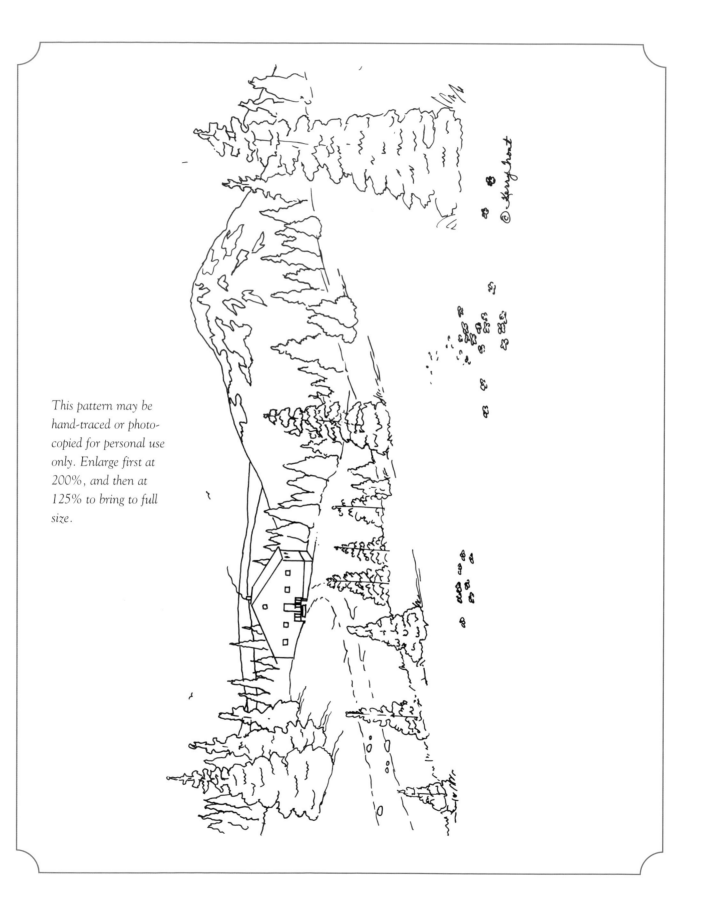

This pattern may be hand-traced or photo-copied for personal use only. Enlarge first at 200%, and then at 125% to bring to full size.

1 Before you distress and paint the shelf, this is how it will look. The wooden section inside of the shelf frame is the insert, which is removable. You will be removing this insert to paint the shelf and to paint the landscape.

2 Remove the insert and set aside. Sand the shelf well and fill in any nail holes with wood filler.

3 Lightly sand the filler with a Teflon pad.

4 Use my rock 'n roll technique to age the shelf. Simply roll a large rock over the surface and against the edges. The rock needs to be rough and a bit jagged to work well. This is better (and quieter!) than beating the shelf with a chain. A chain leaves uniform marks, whereas the rock couldn't possibly. Roll the rock on the shelf area only.

SKY AND MOUNTAINS

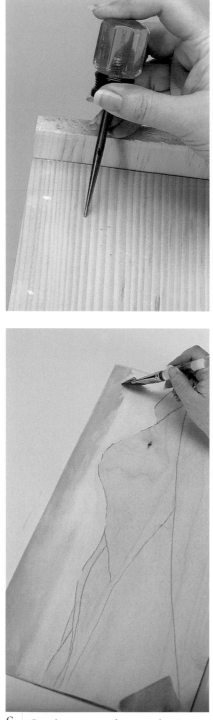

5 | Add the appearance of worm-holes on the shelf by pressing a sharp awl ⅛ inch (0.3cm) into the wood at a slight angle. Real wormholes are telltale signs of old wood, so this is just another way to add age to your piece. Even though we will paint this shelf, the wormholes will still show.

Now use your X-Acto knife to carve out random scallops from the edges of the shelf. This will also help make the piece look worn.

Mix DecoArt Clear Gel Stain and Milk Chocolate (1:1) to make about 3 ounces of mix. Apply the gel stain to the shelf as you would any other wood stain, brushing it on in sections and then wiping it off. Your finish does not have to look perfect because you will cover it with paint anyway.

When dry, rub a wax stick over the edges of the shelf, around the pegs and onto the flat surfaces. If you don't have a wax stick, a white candle, canning paraffin, or even a bit of paste car wax will work the same way. Later, this little trick will allow the paint to come off easily where you want it to.

After waxing, paint the shelf with two coats of Americana Satins Birch Bark, allowing two hours between coats. Set aside to dry.

See step 40 for instructions on finishing the shelf after it is dry.

6 | On the removed insert, begin tracing on the mountains, hills and sky. Using your 1-inch (25mm) flat, block in the sky with Blue Chiffon. Also deepen the sky with Baby Blue and blend any hard edges.

7 | With your ½-inch (12mm) flat, basecoat the distant mountains with Titanium White and Country Blue mixed 2:1.

8 | Basecoat the middle area of the mountain range using a 1:1 mix of Titanium White and Country Blue with the same brush.

9 | Using your 1-inch (25mm) flat, block in the foreground mountain with Country Blue.

10 Mix Titanium White and Country Blue (6:1) with your palette knife. Add snow to the shaded side of the mountains by wiping the palette knife through the paint, then wiping it against the side of your palette so there is just a thin film of paint left on the knife. Hold the knife almost flat against the surface, and with light pressure run the knife against the surface, almost as if buttering bread. The paint will come off the knife in irregular strokes and will simulate snow on a jagged mountainside.

11 Add snow to the sunlit side of the mountains with Titanium White in the same way as in step 10.

12 Block in the left hill with Olive Green and Avocado (6:1) using your 1-inch (25mm) flat. Shade the top of the meadow with Black Green and blend the colors using your ½-inch (12mm) flat.

13 Place a shadow on the left side of the meadow also using Black Green and the same two brushes as in step 12. Blend the colors as you move to the right. Let dry. Trace on the lodge. Stroke in the tree trunks with Black Green using your no. 2 liner.

14 Stipple in the background pine trees with Black Green using a small scruffy brush.

TREES AND LODGE

15 Stroke in the foreground tree trunks with Milk Chocolate using your no. 2 liner. With your small scruffy brush, stipple Avocado trees on top of the Black Green tree line to add depth to your painting.

16 With the same brush, stipple in the foreground trees with a dry-brush mix of Black Green and Avocado. Paint the foreground trees darker by using less Avocado on your brush as you advance.

17 Still using your small scruffy, highlight the trees with a 1:1 mix of Avocado and Olive Green.

18 Reapply the pattern and trace on the lodge. With your ¼-inch (6mm) flat shader and Driftwood, block in the lodge. Let dry; then apply another coat. Mix Titanium White with a touch of Lamp Black to make a very light gray and using the same brush, basecoat the roof.

19 To paint the horizontal beams, use painter's tape and tape off the front section of the lodge (you will be covering the right outside wall of the lodge at this time). This will allow you to pull your brush across the building in a fluid movement and maintain the sharp edges of the corner.

20 Brush mix Driftwood, Lamp Black and Milk Chocolate with water for a very thin deep gray-brown. Use your no. 1 liner to pull horizontal beams. Allow to dry and remove the tape.

21 Tape off the furthest corner of the lodge as shown, and with the same brush and mix, add the beams on the right side of the lodge. Angle the beams parallel to the eaves of the roof to give the building perspective.

22 Remove the tape and basecoat the windows with Lamp Black and Titanium White (1:1) using your 5/0 round. Using the same brush, basecoat the door with a dry-brush mix of Driftwood, Lamp Black and Milk Chocolate. Also basecoat the chimney with Milk Chocolate.

23 Streak in the highlights on the windowpanes using your 5/0 round with a drybrush of Titanium White. Use the same brush to apply Driftwood and Titanium White (1:1) to the windowsills, the right side of the windows, the right side of the door, the left side of the chimney and on the left eave of the roof.

Using Milk Chocolate on your 5/0 round, create patches of rust on the roof. Highlight the front of the eaves using Driftwood and Titanium White (1:1) using your 5/0 round. Drybrush the same mix onto the foundation.

24 Shade the left side and the top of the windows with Lamp Black and Milk Chocolate (1:1) on your 5/0 round. Use the same mixture to shade the left side and top of the door. Thin the mix and add a shadow under the eaves of the roof and to the base of the chimney on the right side using your 5/0 round. Add more water to the thinned mix and wash over the side of the lodge. This should be a watery, translucent wash and should not obscure the building details.

FOREGROUND

25 Add birds using a mix of Lamp Black and Milk Chocolate (1:1) with your no. 1 liner. With Titanium White on your no. 1 round, swirl on the smoke and immediately damp blend it out. Concentrate the smoke at the base of the chimney and gradually blend into the sky as it moves further away.

26 Reapply the pattern and trace on the path and the porch. Lighten the grass area in front of the lodge using Olive Green plus a touch of Titanium White with your no. 8 flat shader. With the chisel edge of the brush, stroke in this mixture to "plant" grass into the meadow. Drybrush a few highlights along the sides of the path using the same mixture. Use the full side of your no. 8 flat to block in the path using slightly curved brushstrokes of Driftwood.

27 Drybrush highlights on the right side of the path in random spots using your no. 8 flat shader and Driftwood, plus a touch of Titanium White. Place the chisel edge of your brush on the right side of the path; then sweep inward toward the path center. Make the path lighter as it gets closer to the lodge; then blend it in with the grass near the building. Use the same brush to pick up thinned Avocado and run an irregular, jagged line against the left side of the path. This adds a bit of height to the grass along the path. Pull a few brushstrokes higher toward the end of the path. With thinned Olive Green and Black Green (1:1), use your no. 8 flat and starting at the base of the trees, pull shadows down toward the path. Follow the contour of the land.

28 Reapply the pattern and trace on the rocks. Use your 5/0 round to block them in using Driftwood with a touch of Titanium White. Once dry, highlight the left side of the rocks with Titanium White. Shade the stones on the right side using a thinned mix of Driftwood plus a touch of Lamp Black. In order to preserve the illusion of the round objects, highlight and shading must never touch and must always be separated by a middle value.

Use thinned Milk Chocolate with a touch of Lamp Black on your no. 8 flat to create the shadow of the tree where it has crossed the path. Also shade the left side of the path where the grass would cast a shadow. Add cast shadows on the ground to the right side of each rock with the same mixture. With your 5/0 round, paint a more concentrated line of Milk Chocolate for the shadow where each rock sits on the ground.

29 Basecoat the foreground grass area with Avocado on your 1-inch (25mm) flat. Allow to dry. Brush on the Brush 'n Blend extender over the Avocado and blend in patches of Black Forest Green.

30 Brush Olive Green onto the grass area and blend as you go, using the same brush.

31 Add the porch using a dry-brush mix of Driftwood and Lamp Black with your 5/0 round. With the same Lamp Black and Milk Chocolate mix used to shade the eaves (step 24) add the porch shadows.

32 Add Titanium White to the porch base mix and highlight the porch using your 5/0 round.

33 To add the foreground tree, paint the trunk using Black Green on your no. 1 liner. Use the same color to stipple branches on with your small scruffy brush.

34 Mix Black Green and Avocado 1:1; then stipple this onto the branches.

35 Stipple straight Avocado onto the front left side of the tree. Cover less of an area than in the previous step.

36 Mix Avocado and Olive Green 1:1 and stipple, again covering a smaller area than before. Finally, stipple straight Olive Green very sparingly on a few branches. Paint cast shadows onto the ground from the base of the tree with your ¼-inch flat.

37 Add a few five-petal flowers to the foreground using Titanium White for the petals and Golden Straw for the centers. Just dot these in with your no. 2 liner. Also, using your no. 2 liner, you can add some blades of grass using various shades of green. Once your project is thoroughly dry, seal it with DecoArt DuraClear Exterior/Interior Varnish using the 1-inch (25mm) flat or foam brush. Dry thoroughly.

Scruffy brushes are simply brushes that are worn out and have lost their shape (I always use an old round brush). They are perfect for stippling. When stippling color onto your surface, load the scruffy with the paint; then pounce the brush onto a paper towel to make the bristles spread out. If you don't do this on a paper towel first, your first pounce will be a blob of paint.

The varnish should only be stirred. Never shake the bottle because this will create air bubbles. If bubbles appear on your painting, blow on them and they will disappear.

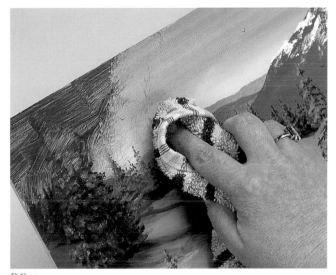

38 Mix DecoArt Clear Gel Stain with Milk Chocolate (3:1). Apply the stain to a section of the insert using your 1-inch (25mm) foam brush.

39 Use a clean rag to lightly rub the stain off in a circular motion. Leave more stain in the corners. (To remove more of the antiquing, use a dampened rag.)

40 When your shelf is thoroughly dry (overnight is best), use the Teflon pad to sand the edges of the shelf. The paint should come off easily in the areas where you applied wax. The dark stained wood will show through. Antique the shelf as instructed in steps 38 and 39.

Finally with a clean rag, smear dark brown antiquing wax (paste shoe polish works great, too!) in different places on the surface of the shelf. This adds a different kind of "dirt" to the shelf. Replace the painted insert once it has dried. With the faux aging techniques you've now learned, your shelf will appear old and rustic.

Tuscany Hatbox

Hatboxes are big in decorating these days. And because of this, they are coming out of the attic and into antique stores and flea markets. Most people want the boxes for their nostalgic look, but when I found this big oval box, I immediately saw it as an empty canvas!

If you want to try this project, be sure to choose a hatbox with heavy cardboard construction.

MATERIALS

BRUSHES no. 18/0 liner, no. 1 script liner, no. 2 script liner, no. 1 round, no. 2 round, no. 3 round, ¼-inch (6mm) flat, ½-inch (12mm) flat, no. 12 flat, ¼-inch (6mm) mop, small scruffy, medium scruffy **ADDITIONAL SUPPLIES** 2 small sea sponges, white transfer paper, painter's glaze, gesso, DuraClear Satin Varnish, latex or plastic gloves **SURFACE** heavy cardboard hatbox from a craft or variety store or flea market

PAINTS = DecoArt Americana

Slate Grey + Light Avocado (3:1) | Black Green | Avocado | Raw Sienna

Slate Grey | Titanium White | Milk Chocolate | Light Avocado

Jade Green | Dioxazine Purple | Deep Periwinkle | Wisteria

Golden Straw | Payne's Grey | Sand | Honey Brown

Cashmere Beige | Blue Mist | Buttermilk

PLACING THE COLUMNS

1 | Apply gesso to the outside of the box and lid according to label directions. This will help add stability to your box and give you a better surface to work with. Gesso can be sanded smooth, but I kept my brushstrokes visible to add texture to my piece.

When dry, replace the lid and draw a fine pencil line around the box lid to indicate the edge. This will determine where the tops of the columns will be placed.

2 | To figure how many columns will fit around your surface, measure your box circumference and divide it by 6 inches (15cm) which is the desired space between columns. My hatbox is 42 inches (107cm) around, so I spaced out seven columns 6 inches (15cm) apart. If you have an odd-size box, you can space the columns an inch either way. The number of columns is not as important as getting them evenly spaced apart.

3 | The space at the bottom of the box for the ledge that the columns would sit on depends on the height of your box. Make the ledge at least the depth of the rim of the box top. To make the ledge the same depth as the rim of the box, place the lid on the bottom of the box and draw a pencil line around it just as you did for the top. Adjust the height of the columns so that they rest on the top and bottom lines by adding or taking out space in the straight part of the columns.

Once you have determined the height of your columns, trace one column onto card stock and cut out a pattern to trace around. Then trace all the columns so that they rest on the top and bottom pencil lines.

Use a large sponge to paint the lid of the box, columns and ledge with Sand, then allow to dry.

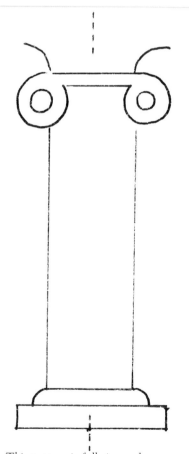

This pattern is full size and may be hand-traced or photocopied for personal use only.

4 When using a sponge, you may want to wear gloves to prevent your hands from getting covered with paint. Mix glaze and Cashmere Beige (1:2) and with a damp sea sponge, apply randomly over the Sand. Immediately diffuse, or soften, that color with another clean, damp sponge. You will retain the sponged look, but it will be soft and mottled.

For the columns, switch to your small scruffy to apply the glaze mix then diffuse it with a small sponge. Be sure to carry the color beyond the pencil lines so that the entire column has a uniform stucco look. Any overpainting will be concealed later by the sky.

5 Mix glaze with Honey Brown (2:1). Apply this to the lid, rim, columns and the ledge under the columns, using the technique described in step 4. Apply this glaze with a lighter touch than you did with the Cashmere Beige.

6 Mix glaze and Sand (2:1) and apply to the same areas and in the same manner as you did the glazes in the previous two steps. At this point, the diffusing sponge may start to remove previous color. This is normal and expected and adds to the texture of the stucco.

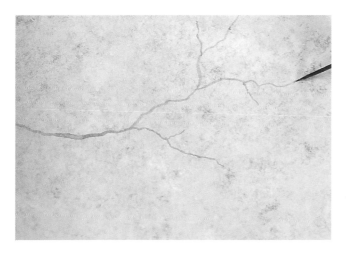

7 Use your no. 2 liner loaded with thinned Milk Chocolate to drag out small, irregular "cracks" in the stucco. Lay your brush almost flat with just the tip touching the surface. Then drag and slightly twist the brush to help the line look irregular. It helps to have a shaky hand when you're applying cracks.

PAINTING THE COLUMNS

Buttermilk highlights

Buttermilk highlights

Extend (overpaint) stucco colors beyond lines

Background colors will conceal overpainting.

Raw Sienna shading

Deeper shading

8 With your no. 2 round, apply Buttermilk highlights to the left and to the upper edges that would catch light, including the ridges in the scrollwork.

9 Apply Raw Sienna to all the shaded areas on the right. With your no. 2 round, shade the scrollwork. Keep the shadows rounded.

10 Use Milk Chocolate and your no. 2 round to add deeper shadows. Do this only where the Raw Sienna is already applied.

11 Transfer the patterns for the niche and decorative frieze onto the hatbox lid. Center as best you can depending on the shape and size of your hatbox. The niche is a recessed shelf with a curved back wall, and it will be shaded to look convincingly dimensional and concave. The light is coming from the upper left, so the left side wall of the niche should appear darker than the much-lighter right side.

Load your ½-inch (12mm) flat shader with Milk Chocolate. Starting at the left side of the shelf, shade up the inner edge of the left wall, then taper off before the midway point at the top of the arch. Wipe the brush and blend the shading toward the center back wall. Don't bring the shading any further across the back wall than the midway point.

Allow to dry completely; then reapply the shading but don't extend the blend as far as you did for the first application. This second application deepens the shadow.

This pattern may be hand-traced or photocopied for personal use only. Enlarge at 200% to bring it up to full size.

This pattern may be hand-traced or photocopied for personal use only. Enlarge at 200% and then at 167% to bring it up to full size.

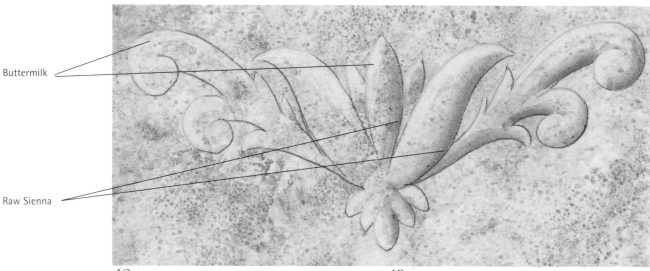

Buttermilk

Raw Sienna

12 Use your no. 3 round brush to apply Buttermilk highlights to the upper-left edges of the sculpture. Diffuse the inside edge of the highlight toward the center.

13 With your ¼-inch (6mm) flat, float Raw Sienna on the lower right edges of the sculpture to create shading. The elements should begin to look round and dimensional. Remember: the base color always separates the highlight and shade colors. If those colors would meet, it would kill the illusion of dimension.

Buttermilk

Thinned
Raw Sienna

Full-strength
Raw Sienna

14 Use your no. 2 round with thinned Raw Sienna to create shadows in the creases and on the lower right sides of the sculpture. Damp blend this color to diffuse any hard edges. When dry, use full strength Raw Sienna in the deepest shadows.

15 Apply Buttermilk with your no. 1 round on the top edges where the pattern lines show through. Any pattern lines on the lower edges should be covered by the Raw Sienna.

16 With your no. 1 liner, apply Raw Sienna on the outer bands and on the lower right sides of the frieze design.

17 With the same brush, paint Buttermilk on the upper left edges of the frieze design and paint bands above the bands of Raw Sienna. Make sure the paint is thick enough to cover the pattern lines.

LANDSCAPE

This pattern may be hand-traced or photocopied for personal use only. It appears here at full size.

18 Transfer the landscape pattern to the area between each of the columns. Add interest to the landscape by changing the basic pattern so that each of the sections are not exactly the same.

Basecoat the sky area with Blue Mist using your no. 12 flat. Allow to dry. Create the transparent distant clouds with glaze and Titanium White mixed 4:1 using your ¼-inch (6mm) mop. Pounce the color on lightly, then wipe the brush and soften the edges of the clouds.

When painting sky and land, outline the columns in the corresponding color using your no. 2 round then fill in the larger areas with your no. 12 flat. Using the smaller brush to first outline the columns will help you to maintain a straight edge, and will also help keep the sky color from overlapping onto the columns.

19 Build another layer of clouds by adding a touch more Titanium White to the glaze mix.

20 With your ¼-inch (6mm) mop, highlight the upper left corner of the clouds with the glaze mix from step 19 plus a touch more Titanium White.

21 To clean up the bottoms of the clouds, horizontally brush a very thin mix of glaze plus Titanium White across the bottoms of the clouds using your no. 12 flat.

Mix Titanium White and Jade Green (2:1) and brush in the distant horizon line by slightly angling your no. 12 flat. Angling the brush will reduce the width of the brush stroke.

22 Mix Jade Green with a touch of Avocado and using your no. 12 flat, stroke in the area forward of and down slightly from the horizon line. These strokes should appear streaky.

23 Still using your no. 12 flat, create the gently rolling hills by adding more Avocado to the mix, then continue with horizontal strokes down the surface. Vary the shades of green as you move down the surface, going darker as you go down. End with Avocado. This gradation of color helps simulate distance.

24 Use your no. 1 round to paint in the base of distant foliage. Simply begin with a horizontal line that follows the slope of the land. Then stipple the rest of the trees in as shown. Remember the clumps of trees will get larger as they come forward in the picture. Pounce in the distant trees with Avocado using your no. 1 round.

LANDSCAPE, *continued*

25 Add the trunks for the Lombardy Poplars with Avocado and your no. 2 liner. Draw smaller trunks for the distant trees.

26 Working from the bottom to the top, stipple in the distant trees with Avocado using the small scruffy. Using your medium scruffy, stipple in the foreground trees with a mix of Avocado a touch of Black Green.

27 Highlight the left side of the distant trees with a mix of Titanium White plus Avocado using your small scruffy. Highlight the foreground trees with Avocado plus a touch of Jade Green using the medium scruffy. Be sure the highlight for the foreground trees is darker than the highlight on the distant trees.

WISTERIA

28 Mix Black Green and Avocado 1:2 for a deep green. With your no. 1 script liner, paint a few winding vines around a column or two and up under the inside edge of the roof. With the same mix, stipple foliage onto the vines with your small scruffy. Use the same brush and stipple Light Avocado onto the left side of the foliage.

29 Mix Deep Periwinkle with a touch of Payne's Grey for a medium plum color. With your small scruffy, stipple blooms onto the vine. Wisteria hangs like clusters of grapes, so make the blossoms point downward.

Add Titanium White to the first color to achieve a very light lavender color. With your small scruffy, stipple this onto the left side of the wisteria blossoms.

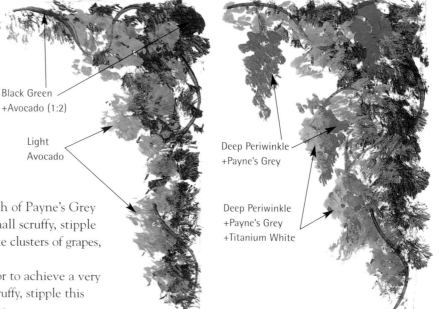

Black Green +Avocado (1:2)

Light Avocado

Deep Periwinkle +Payne's Grey

Deep Periwinkle +Payne's Grey +Titanium White

30 Center the urn pattern into the niche, then transfer. Mix Slate Grey and Light Avocado (3:1) and basecoat the urn. Use your ½-inch (12mm) flat for the body and the ¼-inch (6mm) flat for the handles and mouth of the urn.

31 Mix Payne's Grey and Black Green (2:1) and float this around all sides of the urn. Use your ½-inch (12mm) flat on the body and the ¼-inch (6mm) flat on the handles and mouth. An old urn might be hand-made from clay and have flaws and irregularities, so this should be a rough float. Apply a heavier float to the right side of the urn.

32 With your medium scruffy, dry-brush patches of thinned Raw Sienna, Avocado, and the Payne's Grey/Black Green mix onto the lower right side of the urn. Use a very dry brush to give the urn this rustic texture (and to make it look a bit mossy).

33 Use the same brush to drybrush Titanium White onto the upper left side of the urn, handles and mouth. The highlight must be just as rough-looking as the shading, since the urn would have the same texture all over. Load your 18/0 liner with the Payne's Grey/Black Green mix and add a few cracks to the vessel. Also deepen the shadows under the rim and handles. Use your small scruffy to lightly add a few spots of Avocado and Raw Sienna onto the handles and mouth.

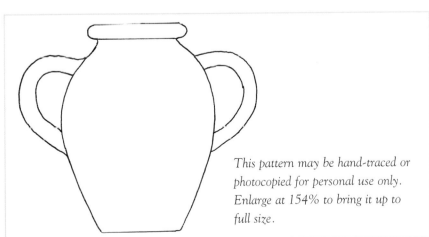

This pattern may be hand-traced or photocopied for personal use only. Enlarge at 154% to bring it up to full size.

IRISES

34 | Line up the pattern with the urn and transfer the irises onto the lid. Using your no. 2 round, paint the leaves Avocado. Still using the same brush, shade the right side and the base of the leaves with Avocado and a touch of Black Green. Also highlight the left edges of the leaves with a mix of Jade Green and a touch of Titanium White.

Switch to your 18/0 liner loaded with the same color thinned. Paint very long, straight veins on the leaves going from the base up to the tip. Make each stroke very fine.

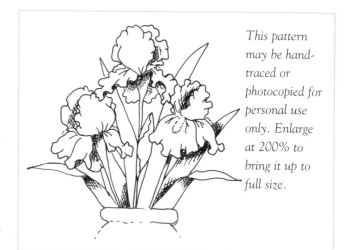

This pattern may be hand-traced or photocopied for personal use only. Enlarge at 200% to bring it up to full size.

35 | With your ¼-inch (6mm) flat shader, paint the lower petals Deep Periwinkle and the upper ones Wisteria. Paint the stem and calyx Light Avocado and highlight the same way as you did the leaves. Make them darker (as instructed in step 36) where they are shaded by the flower petals.

With your no. 2 round, shade the lower petals with thinned Payne's Grey near the base of the petal and underneath the petal. Notice how this color under the back petals makes them recede and gives the flowers depth. Put a bit of this color at the base of the upper petals, and also underneath the edges of the lower petals where the ruffles expose the underneath. Define the ruffles on the upper side of the petals with this same color. With a thinned Deep Periwinkle, shade the upper petals at the base and on the back petal.

Use your ¼-inch (6mm) flat to float thinned Dioxazine Purple around the ruffled edges of all the petals. Then use your no. 1 round to run a line of the same color around the edge and also perpendicular to the edges to suggest folds and ruffles.

36 | Using your no. 2 round, drybrush thinned Titanium White onto the middle area of the upper petals to help round them out. With the same brush, highlight the high parts of the ruffles with this color also. Use your 18/0 liner to paint a very fine line of thinned Wisteria around the edges of the bottom petals. This will help define the petals against their dark background. Use your no. 1 round to stipple Honey Brown onto the lower petals to make a fuzzy stamen "tongue." Highlight with Golden Straw. At the base of the tongue, shade the petal with thinned Payne's Grey. Use your 18/0 liner and Payne's Grey to paint very fine veins out from the base of the bottom petals.

37 When your hatbox is complete, apply two coats of DuraClear Satin Varnish. Lining the box with beautiful fabric—such as brocade or quilted satin—would be an elegant way to finish it out.

Make sure the brush you use for varnishing is clean and free of any dust or old paint.

Trompe L'oeil Cat

I wanted to paint a mini-mural over a window—something different and unexpected. I also wanted something for all of my readers who have asked me for cat projects. So my friend here seemed a good choice. And isn't it just like a cat to love being up high? He's also painted to be an illusion, because I have painted him to make the wall look deeper than it is. Paint this silky Siamese above your window or door and anyone who sees it is sure to do a double take!

MATERIALS

BRUSHES ½-inch (12mm) flat, ¼-inch (6mm) flat, rake brush, large scruffy brush, large mop brush, no. 2 round, no. 2 script liner **ADDITIONAL SUPPLIES** toothpick, transfer paper **SURFACE** painted wall

PAINTS = DecoArt Americana

Cashmere Beige	Toffee	Buttermilk	Sable Brown

Burnt Umber	Bittersweet Chocolate	DeLane's Dark Flesh	Light Buttermilk

Titanium White	Soft Black	Blueberry	Desert Sand

Lamp (Ebony) Black   Kerry's Liquid Shadow

UNDERCOAT

This pattern may be hand-traced or photocopied for personal use only. Enlarge at 200% to bring it up to full size.

©Kerry Trout

1 Decide where you want to place the mural and trace on the pattern using transfer paper. To check the spacing and angle of the eyes and to make sure lines are okay after the pattern was transferred, hold a ruler parallel to the angle of the face, and draw a line between the eyes. The corners of the eyes should line up.

Using your ½-inch (12mm) flat brush, undercoat the body and around the face with Cashmere Beige. Undercoat the inside of the ears with DeLane's Dark Flesh. While the first coat is drying, add the cast shadow on the left side of the cat using Kerry's Liquid Shadow mixture. Dab the shadow mixture on with your large scruffy brush and then diffuse with your large mop brush.

Add a second coat of the undercoat colors. Soften the outer edges of the Cashmere Beige all the way around with a dry ½-inch (12mm) brush.

2 | Mix DeLane's Dark Flesh with a little bit of Burnt Umber, then with your no. 2 round paint the outside edges of the ears. Damp blend into the pink with your ¼-inch (6mm) flat brush. Then outline the ears with Burnt Umber using your no. 2 round.

3 | Still using your no. 2 round, define the ears by lightly stroking Sable Brown on top of the Burnt Umber. Mix a small amount of Soft Black and Burnt Umber (1:1) and with your no. 2 liner draw some little hairs coming out of the ears. (The paint for the hairs must be extremely thin.) Do the same with Cashmere Beige mixed with Burnt Umber (1:1).

4 | Use your ½-inch (12mm) flat to undercoat the paws and the tail with Soft Black. On the tail, use your ¼-inch (6mm) flat and a drybrush technique to feather out the edges. You want to prevent any hard lines.

If you are going to paint the cat over a door frame or over a window frame like I did, extend the leg over the edge just a little bit.

5 | Now basecoat the cat with Toffee using your ½-inch (12mm) flat. Take this just inside the edge of the Cashmere Beige undercoat. On the left side of the cat the Toffee isn't extended out as far, as that area will be shaded. Use your rake brush to extend the Toffee out onto the Cashmere Beige edge. Just lightly feather out over top of the undercoat that you softened before. Keep the paint on your rake brush very thin.

6 | With your rake brush, continue pulling hairs around the ears further out than anywhere else. The hair on the top of the head is kept flatter than anywhere else.

Using your ½-inch (12mm) brush, apply Buttermilk to the body using short choppy strokes in the direction of the hair growth. This shouldn't be extended all the way out to the edges. Apply this also to the right side only of the cat's face

After this has dried, you can retrace the pattern if you feel it is necessary. Especially make sure you have the lines underneath the chin.

7 | With your rake brush, stroke hairs around the edge of the body with Buttermilk. This time make longer strokes over the chest and make shorter strokes around the jaw area, the forehead, in front of the ears and on the top of the head.

DEFINING THE FUR, FACE

8 Using the same short choppy strokes and your ½-inch (12mm) flat loaded with Light Buttermilk, paint over the Buttermilk area. Be careful to keep the elbow and the back hip area (haunches) defined. Now use your rake brush to paint in the appearance of hair all over the body.

Note: At this point I realized that the hip area seemed too square, so I rounded it off by using the rake brush and stroking on some thinned Cashmere Beige and Burnt Umber (1:1) to redefine the shape.

9 Still using your rake brush, the thinned Cashmere Beige and Burnt Umber (1:1), add some heavy shadowing, especially above the foot, but also in the areas as shown. Start at the foot and stroke upwards. (This area can be pretty dark because it will be covered with more hair later.)

Also add some of this mixture to the face. Right now, don't worry about feathering where the lighter hair meets the tail.

10 Using your rake brush, soften the shadows with strokes of the Light Buttermilk. Use soft strokes.

It's important to keep your strokes smooth and consistent. This will, in turn, create a smooth coat on the cat. Make sure you make the strokes go in the direction that the hair grows.

11 Mix Titanium White and Light Buttermilk (1:1) and with your rake brush, go over the hair again. Stay to the midsection to help create the round form (dimension) in your painting. Also fill in the neck area with the same mixture.

12 Still using your rake brush and Titanium White, create a highlight effect by filling in even less of the body area.

Use Burnt Umber and Titanium White (1:2) (which will create a mushroom color) and your rake brush to soften the area where the dark and light colors meet.

Go over these edges a second time softening and blending even more.

13 Undercoat the face with Soft Black using your ¼-inch (6mm) flat. Even though you are just undercoating, feather out your strokes. Feather from the nose out.

You will need two coats of the Soft Black. Go around the eyes and leave a little of the pattern line open for the nose.

14 After this dries, go over the same area with Burnt Umber using your ¼-inch (6mm) flat. Use Sable Brown with your rake brush to add hairs to the outside edge of the Burnt Umber. They can overlap the Burnt Umber.

Add a little more color to the left side as this is the shadow side.

15 Do the same thing using your ½-inch (12mm) flat with Sable Brown. This will soften and blend the Burnt Umber and the Sable Brown.

16 Next use Bittersweet Chocolate with a touch of Titanium White and starting at the nose, brush up the bridge and blend into the forehead, below the eyes and around the upper part of the mouth.

NOSE

17 Use your no. 2 round with Bittersweet Chocolate and a touch of Titanium White (just enough to make it a dark gray color) to paint the nose leather (the triangle around the edge of the nose).

Use Lamp Black to outline the edge of the nose, the nostrils and the split in the upper lip.

18 Mix a little more Titanium White into the Bittersweet Chocolate to create a lighter gray. With your no. 2 round, apply this around the inside of the left eye using feathery strokes. Highlight the right side of the muzzle with the same color using short choppy strokes.

19 Add a little more Titanium White and highlight the nose, around the edge of the right nostril, up the bridge of the nose and under the eyes a little.

20 Using Sable Brown and your no. 2 round, paint a light wash around the bottom edge of the muzzle, this gives it some roundness. Damp blend this into the area right underneath. To suggest skin, touch DeLane's Dark Flesh into the triangle area, then damp-blend downward.

21 Using your no. 2 round, outline the eyes with Lamp Black. On the lower lid paint a thin line of thinned Sable Brown. Mix Blueberry and Titanium White (2:1) and fill in the eye area. Place a fine Lamp Black line above the upper lid also.

If you would prefer to have different colored or lighter eyes on your cat, feel free to change or adjust the color.

22 Add more Titanium White to the blue mixture and with your no. 2 round, add a line of highlighting along the bottom of the eyeball. Blend this into the darker blue. Add a dot of Lamp Black to straight Blueberry to make a navy blue color. Paint a shadow across the top of the eyeball and damp blend it towards the center. Add more Titanium White to the lighter blue mixture and run just a thin line along the bottom edge of the eyelid. Damp blend.

23 Mix DeLane's Dark Flesh and a little bit of Titanium White to get a medium pink. With your no. 2 round, make a short stroke across the upper part of each eyeball as shown.

24 Add pupils with Lamp Black using the same brush. Use a toothpick with Titanium White to dot in highlights on each side of the pupil and add just a very thin dot on the lower lids. Also add a little speck of Titanium White on the inner corner of each eye.

25 Dot in pores on the muzzle with Lamp Black and your no. 2 liner. Using the same brush and very diluted Titanium White, touch your brush to the pore and pull out the whiskers. Add whiskers right above the eyes to form the eyebrows. (For techniques for painting whiskers, see "Using Your Liner Brush," page 17.)

26 The leg and tail are painted similarly to the face. Use Burnt Umber and your rake brush to brush in hairs on the leg and tail. Use your no. 2 liner to add a little line of Burnt Umber where the leg and body meet.

With your ½-inch (12mm) flat, apply Sable Brown just to the top part of the leg and tail.

27 Use Bittersweet Chocolate and Titanium White (1:1) to highlight the top of the tail and the leg.

28 Right above the corner of the window where the tail and body meet, use your rake brush with Titanium White and brush in hairs to connect the body and tail.

29 Add some shadowing (as described in step 1) with the liquid shadow mixture right below the paw that is sticking out on the front of the windowframe. Add a window dressing and enjoy the wonderful compliments you will receive.

Shaker Clock

Everyone loves grandfather clocks, but we don't all have the room for one. With this project, you can have a grandfather clock by painting it yourself. Look closely—this is a real working clock! I painted this on a small flat door, the kind of door that you might have on a broom closet or linen closet. The door should be a hollow-core door to accommodate the clockworks.

I studied several authentic Shaker clocks to come up with this unadorned, no nonsense design. I feel this design will add interest to any area of your home.

MATERIALS

BRUSHES 5/0 liner, 18/0 liner, no. 1 script liner, no. 2 script liner, 1/4-inch (6mm) flat shader, no. 0 round, no. 1 round, no. 2 round, no. 8 flat, no 12 flat, 1-inch (25mm) flat, 1/2-inch (12mm) mop, small scruffy **ADDITIONAL SUPPLIES** black marker, ballpoint pen, painter's tape, painter's glaze, Scotch tape, light graphite paper, straight-edge, compass, round toothpicks, small scissors, Americana Satins Gloss Varnish, Americana Satins Satin Varnish **SURFACE** 18-inch (46cm) wide flat door from a home goods, hardware or decorating center

PAINTS = DecoArt Americana; Americana Satins (AS)

Lamp (Ebony) Black

Asphaltum

Raw Sienna

Honey Brown

Black Satin (AS)

Country Green (AS)

Graphite

 Titanium White

Gooseberry Pink

Sand

Sage Green (AS)

 Antique Mauve

Black Green

Avocado

Black Plum

 Light Willow (AS)

Antique Mauve+White (2:1)

Antique Mauve+White (1:1)

 Victorian Blue+White (2:1)

Victorian Blue

Victorian Blue+White (1:2)

 Golden Straw

 Soft Black

 Milk Chocolate

 Payne's Grey

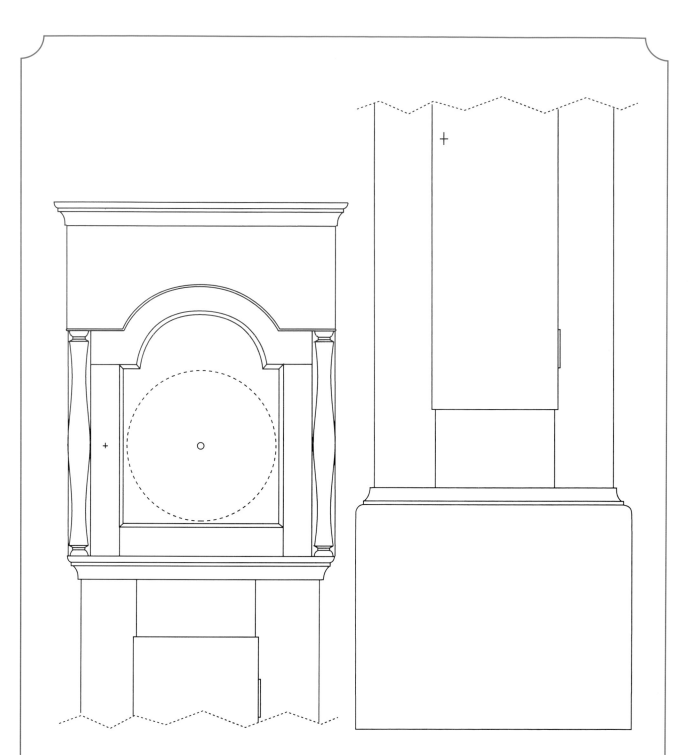

These patterns may be hand-traced or photocopied for personal use only. They must be enlarged three times. Enlarge them first at 200% and a second time at 200% then a third time at 128% to bring them up to full size.

Remove the door if possible. It is much easier to paint this project if the door lies flat. I recommend laying the door across a couple of sawhorses. If the door is painted, you will need to either strip it or rough it up with sandpaper. If the door is unfinished (new) then you need to seal it with wood sealer first.

Next, determine how tall and wide your clock needs to be. Make the clock as tall as space allows. Ideally, you should leave about 6 inches (15cm) for the mouse on top.

Trace the pattern onto tracing paper using a black marker. Enlarge the pattern until the base of the clock is 16 inches (41cm) wide.

Transfer onto your surface the complete outline of the clock and also the outline of the clock face door. Don't worry about the face details at this time. Basecoat the clock with Country Green and let dry.

Be aware of the cracks, edges and doors of the painted clock. Presume that the light is coming from the upper left side. These areas will either catch light or cast a shadow. A crack is recessed, so it needs to be dark. Paint the cracks using a 1:1 mix of Black Satin and Country Green on your no. 2 liner. The right edge of the crack will catch the light, so highlight it with Sage Green using the same liner brush. You'll be amazed at how real your painting looks by putting that very thin stroke of highlight alongside a crack or space.

Your clock won't look authentic unless the paint looks old. To add faux paint imperfections (like stains and dirt), mix just a touch of Black Satin into Country Green, and with your small scruffy, brush it onto areas where dirt would normally accumulate over the years. These would be

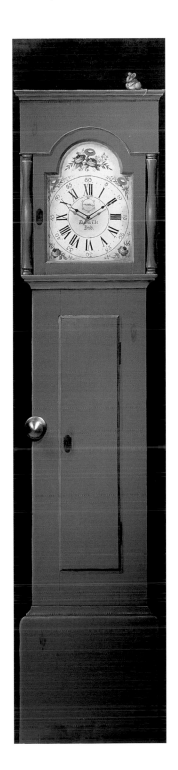

areas such as around the escutcheons, the bottom of the clock, and the bottom of the bonnet door. Make these "stains" very faint.

At the bottom of the clock, stroke from the floor up; this will look like dirt. Another way to age the clock is to reproduce the tannin rings that come through the paint from knots in the wood. Use a medium size round brush with a little bit of very thin Raw Sienna mixed with a touch of Black Satin, and paint a few very faint oblong rings on several areas of the clock (see the upper left side of the clock bonnet).

To shade any surface that would cast a shadow (around the escutcheons, the door, beveled edges, etc.) use a 3:1 mix of Country Green and Black Satin. Use either a ¼-inch (6mm) flat or a no. 1 liner to apply shade.

Transfer the pattern of the escutcheons and hinges. Using your ¼-inch (6mm) flat, shade the beveled edge on the shaded side and bottom of the door with a 2:1 mix of Country Green and Black Satin. Highlight the opposite edges with Sage Green. Add lighter highlights with Light Willow. Use the above shading mixes and highlighting colors to paint the moldings and trim on the clock. Remember that the base color, Country Green, will always separate the shading and highlighting colors. This is how you achieve shape and dimension.

To show the roundness of the molding, float the colors on, then either shade or highlight the opaque end of the float with your no. 2 liner and the appropriate color. In other words, where you float Sage Green against the upper edge of a molding, go back and make it a bit lighter with the lighter color, Light Willow. The same goes for the shading: float on a 2:1 mix of Country Green and Black Satin, and deepen it with Black Green using your no. 2 liner.

ESCUTCHEON

 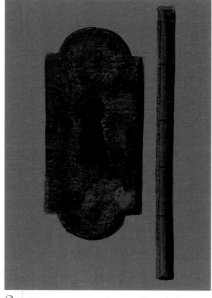 

1 Use your ¼-inch (6mm) flat to basecoat the escutcheon with Asphaltum, and allow to dry. With your small dry scruffy, stipple Raw Sienna onto the escutcheon, and use your no. 2 round to apply it to the highlighted side of the hinge.

2 Use your no. 1 round with Lamp Black to paint the keyhole and to shade the tiny nail heads on either end. Make five very thin horizontal lines evenly spaced across the hinge.

3 Highlight the upper left edges on both items, the right sides of the keyhole, the upper half of the nail heads, and just under each black line on the hinge with the no. 1 round and Honey Brown.

Pendulum door escutcheon

Bonnet door escutcheon

These patterns are full size and may be hand-traced or photocopied for personal use only.

4   Transfer the mouse pattern onto the top of the clock using light graphite paper. Use your ¼-inch (6mm) flat to basecoat the mouse with Graphite, except for the eye and the inside of the ear. With your ¼-inch (6mm) rake or your ¼-inch (6mm) flat, drybrush a mix of Graphite and Titanium White (2:1), using short strokes to simulate fur. On the face, stroke from the nose upward to the forehead and outward to the cheeks. On the body, stroke from his neck around his stomach in the front, and in the back from his neck to the back thigh. On his thigh, start in the middle and stroke outward in each direction, so his thigh looks like a fluffy ball of fur. Be sure to taper off the hairs and pull them out to form tiny hairs that contour the thigh and body too. With the same brush, float Gooseberry Pink around the inside of the ear.

5   Add more Titanium White to the first Graphite mix (see step 4), and using your ¼-inch (6mm) flat (or rake brush) drybrush this lighter gray onto the left side of the body. Also apply it to the left ear, along the bridge of the nose, to his cheek, to the upper sections of the thigh, and to his stomach. Once dry, reapply to his stomach, to make it a bit whiter. Use your no. 1 liner and Lamp Black to outline his nose and front legs. Paint the eye Lamp Black also.

6   Still using the same brush, drybrush more white onto his stomach. Use your small scruffy to drybrush Titanium White onto his front legs. Mix Gooseberry Pink and Graphite (3:1) to get a dark pink (about the color of a pencil eraser), then paint his tail with this mixture. Add a touch more Graphite to the pink mixture and, with your no. 1 liner, make tiny lines at the base of the tail.

With your no. 1 round, paint the left side of the tail where it hangs over the edge, using Gooseberry Pink. This will be the lightest part of the tail; as the rest of it is shaded by the body. Still using your no. 1 liner, add a touch of white to the Gooseberry Pink and add tiny lines across the lighter end of the tail; also float a highlight of this mixture inside of the ear.

Use your 18/0 liner and thinned Titanium White to add very fine whiskers from his muzzle; also add a few over his eyes. Use the same brush to add very fine white highlights around the eyes, and add a speck of reflected light onto the eyeball. Rinse your brush and use Graphite to pull tiny hairs out from the head. These hairs should overlap the ears just a bit. Add more hairs anyplace else you need him to look a bit more furry.

This pattern may be hand-traced or photocopied for personal use only . Enlarge at 143% to bring it up to full size.

CLOCK FACE

7 | To allow the painter's tape in step 8 to mask off the rounded surface, cut slits into the tape. Leave ⅛ inch (0.3) of the tape uncut. As you tape around the edges of the clock face, the slits allow the tape to easily curve to the shape of the clock face.

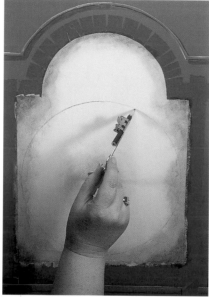

10 | Transfer on the clock face pattern using a ballpoint pen. To aid in transferring on the Roman numerals, use a straightedge.

8 | Tape off the face of the clock. Basecoat the face with Sand using your 1-inch (25mm) flat. Drill a ⅜-inch (1cm) hole for the clockworks in the center of the face. With your ½-inch (12mm) mop brush or any large brush add "dirt" to the face of the clock with a drybrush mix of Milk Chocolate, Payne's Grey and glaze (1:1:2). Start in the middle of the face at the hole and work outward a bit. Also apply it into the corners and edges of the face. Once the mix is applied, mop it off with another dry ½-inch (12mm) mop brush. Apply a second layer of the brush mix to the four corners.

9 | Apply a small piece of Scotch tape over the hole. Center the needle of your compass in the hole, pressing a small hole in the tape to prevent the compass from moving. Use your compass to draw the circle of the clock face. Your compass should be set at 4⅛ inches (10.5cm). This will make your circle 9¼ inches (23.5cm) in diameter. You must trace the circle dark enough to be able to see it through the pattern; this will help you to align your pattern.

11 | This is how the clock will look once you have traced on the pattern.

This pattern may be hand-traced or photocopied for personal use only. Enlarge at 200% then again at 143% to bring it up to full size.

12 Paint all the leaves and stems of the flowers in mixed values of Avocado and Titanium White. Use your no. 2 script liner for the long stems and larger leaves, and for the small leaves use your no. 1 round.

13 Using your no. 8 flat, add the rose leaves with a double load of Avocado and Titanium White.

14   For the shadows under the leaves, float Black Green on your no. 8 flat. For this project I chose to maintain the traditional Shaker clock look and do a simpler folk art rose. If you want, you can use the double-loaded brush technique instead. The pattern will work for both techniques. Using your no. 8 flat, basecoat the roses with three coats of Antique Mauve. Use the same brush to float Black Plum in the bowl of the rose. Also paint the left three-fourths of the rose using a mix of Antique Mauve and Titanium White (2:1).

15   Using your no. 8 flat, load the brush with Antique Mauve and Titanium White (1:1). Stroke in the rose petal highlights using the sharp chisel edge of your loaded brush. Stay within the previous color (previous petals); do not extend beyond them.

16   Add a few more crescent-shaped highlights to the rose with straight Titanium White using your no. 8 flat.

17   Make three dip dots in the center of the roses with Antique Mauve and Titanium White (2:1) using the tip of a toothpick.

18   With your no. 8 flat, basecoat the morning glories with a streaky mix of Victorian Blue and Titanium White (2:1).

19   Highlight the bowl of the flowers with Titanium White using your no. 3 round. Stroke in the "smile."

20   Still using your no. 3 round, pull some streaks out from the smile.

21   With your no. 8 flat, float Victorian Blue right below the white highlight.

22   Dot the centers with Golden Straw using the tip of a toothpick. Paint the throat of the flower Victorian Blue using your no. 1 round.

23   Add the calyx to the morning glories with Avocado using your no. 1 round.

24 Create the pull petals of the small flowers with a mix of Victorian Blue and Titanium White (1:2) using your no. 1 round.

25 Dot the centers with Golden Straw. Add tendrils with diluted Avocado on your no. 1 round. Notice how close to the ferrule I hold the brush. This gives me better control when using small brushes.

26 Using your 18/0 liner and Soft Black, outline the large circle, the Roman numerals, and the smaller circle. Use your no. 0 round for the Arabic numbers and a toothpick for the small dots.

27 Create a mix of Milk Chocolate, Payne's Grey and Victorian Blue. Use your no. 12 flat to wash a shadow on the left side of the clock face. You could also use Kerry's Liquid Shadow mixture for this.

28 Remove the painter's tape carefully. Apply Americana Satins Sage Green on the bottom edge of the clock face door frame using your 5/0 liner.

29 Don't forget to personalize your clock. You can add your last name, a wedding date, or your hometown on it, as I did. To use the pattern, cut a small piece of tracing paper, about 3 inches x 6 inches (7.6 cm x 15.2cm)—or enough to accommodate the name; draw a light pencil mark across the bottom of it with a straightedge. This will be your baseline. Now place this paper over the letter pattern, and trace each letter you need, making sure each one is lined up on the baseline. Space your letters evenly. When done, find the center of your word. Do so by measuring the length of the word and dividing that by two. Find that midpoint and mark it on your pattern. This mark is what you will use to line up with the center hole. Use a level if you need to ensure straight letters.

Transfer the name onto the clock. Paint the letters with your 18/0 liner and Black Satin paint.

With your no. 1 liner and Asphaltum, make small lines of wear along the edges of the clock body, on corners, and anywhere the paint might wear off on a real old clock like this.

a b c d e f g h i j k l m n
o p q r s t u v w x y z
A B C D E F G H I
J K L M N O P Q
R S T U V W X Y Z

These patterns may be hand-traced or photocopied for personal use only. You can increase or decrease the pattern size as dictated by your chosen personalization.

SPINDLES

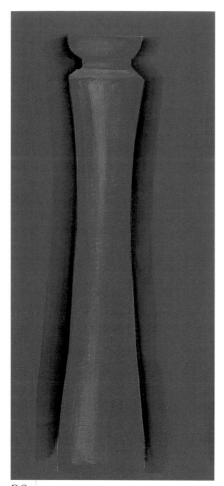

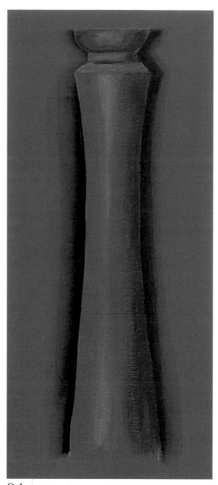

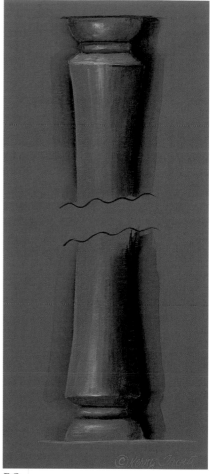

30 | With your no. 12 flat, paint the spindles Country Green. Use Sage Green to lighten the areas and edges of the spindle that would catch the light. The lightest area is along the center-left side of the piece. Use your ¼-inch (6mm) flat for this, and add a touch of Country Green to help blend this color in.

31 | Mix Country Green and Black Green (3:1) to get a dark mossy green. With your no. 8 flat, shade the right side of the spindles and the creases with this mixture.

32 | Add Black Green to the Country Green (1:2) to deepen the shading on the right side. Blend toward the center of the spindle. Use your no. 2 liner to paint this darker color into the creases. The space beside the right side of the spindle is deeply shaded, so the right side of the spindles will blend into this darkest shadow. On the left side, run a 1:1 mix of Country Green and Sage Green using your no. 1 liner along the very edge. Drybrush final light highlights with your ¼-inch (6mm) flat using Light Willow. Still using your no. 1 liner, apply tiny bright highlights to the sharpest edges and the roundest curves.

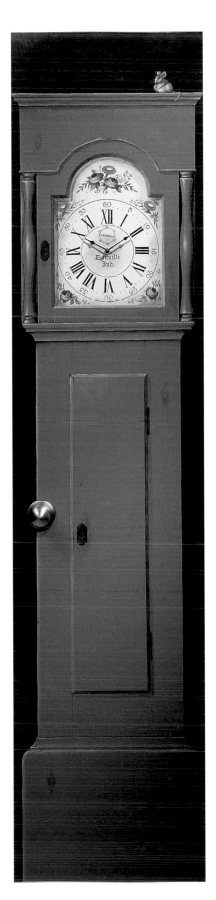

33 Create the appearance of glass over the clock face with Americana Satins Gloss Varnish. Seal the rest of the door with Americana Satins Satin Varnish. Add the hardware, the clock hands and the doorknob.

Trompe L'oeil Wall Shelf

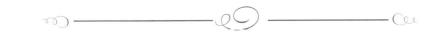

Here's a mini-mural that will fit nicely over a kitchen counter, jelly cabinet, or in that little space where a picture or bric-a-brac just won't do. It is painted to fool the viewer into thinking at first glance that it's real. The illusion is carried off with lots of contrasting shadows and highlights.

I enjoy muraling, and I get a real kick out of painting trompe l'oeil artwork on the wall. It's always so unexpected. Like the Siamese cat in project eight—also painted trompe l'oeil—this mini-mural is sure to take anyone by surprise.

MATERIALS

BRUSHES no. 1 script liner, no. 2 script liner, 1/4-inch (6mm) flat, 1/2-inch (12mm) flat, 3/4-inch (19mm) flat, 1-inch (25mm) flat, no. 8 flat, 10/0 round, no. 2 round, no. 3 round, no. 5 round, 1/4-inch (6mm) mop, no. 6 mop **ADDITIONAL SUPPLIES** tracing paper, compass, graphite paper, painter's tape, toothpick, clear plastic ruler, level, Q-tips, water-based polyurethane spray **SURFACE** painted wall

PAINTS = DecoArt Americana; Hot Shots (HS)

Yellow Light | Soft Black | Avocado | Scorching Yellow (HS)

Hauser Light Green | Lemon Yellow | True Ochre | Neutral Grey

Titanium White | Red Violet | Prussian Blue | Kerry's Liquid Shadow

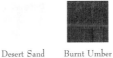

Desert Sand | Burnt Umber | Yellow Ochre | Buttermilk

Arbor Green | Eggshell

Pattern

This pattern may be hand-traced or photocopied for personal use.
Enlarge at 200% and again at 125% to return to full size.

1 Your painting surface should be a light-colored semi-gloss painted wall. Enlarge the pattern so that the shelf width (at the widest point) is 16 inches (41cm). Any trompe l'oeil illusion must be life-size in order to be convincing.

Use large tracing paper or tape several sheets together. Transfer the enlarged pattern onto the tracing paper. Now you have a transparent pattern. Apply graphite paper to the back of the pattern with painter's tape, making sure the dark side is against the wall. It's likely you won't have graphite paper large enough for your pattern. That's okay. Just do what I did and move the graphite paper when you've completed each section.

Position the pattern on the wall where you would like the painting. Tape the pattern at the top in one place. Position the level on the horizontal line of the shelf and make certain your pattern is level. Hold the level lightly against the pattern with one hand and adjust the pattern with your other. The one piece of tape at the top allows the paper to move. When you have the transparent pattern level, hold it flat and tape it in place. Leave about 1 inch (2.5cm) of the tracing paper showing above the graphite paper to allow for registration marks.

Since this is a pattern you will have to reposition a few times, you'll need to make registration marks. With the pattern taped to the wall, make two tiny dots (use a pencil) along the top margin area, one in each corner. Now use a straight pin or point of your compass to go through those tiny holes, straight through the pattern and into the wall. Use very little pressure; you're making a mark, not hanging a picture. Now lift the pattern and make two exact pencil marks right on top of the two holes in the wall.

When you remove the pattern, you can always put it back in the same position by lining up those little pencil marks.

Trace on your pattern except for the plate detailing and the details inside of the bottle. The plate will cover up a small section of the bottle; this is okay. It is very helpful to use a compass to trace the circle of the plate.

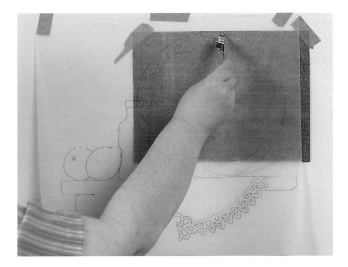

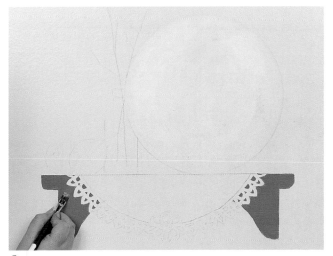

2 Begin by basecoating the plate using your ¾-inch (19mm) flat with a mixture of Titanium White and Eggshell (2:1). This will require two coats; allow to dry between coats.

While the plate is drying, basecoat the shelf with Arbor Green using your ½-inch (12mm) flat. For the little lace eyelets, use your 10/0 round. This will also require two coats of paint.

It is important that you know how to use a level properly. For the novice, when the bubble is centered in the little window directly under the indicator mark, you have a level surface.

3 | In this step you will fill in all of the shadows using Kerry's Liquid Shadow mixture (see page 9).

Beginning with the forsythia shadow, daub the Liquid Shadow on with your no. 5 round brush, then quickly diffuse with your ¼-inch (6mm) mop brush, making any hard edges of the shadow become soft and nondescript. Add the shadow around the plate and around the lemons, shelf and the lace.

4 | Remember to follow with your mop brush as each shadow should have a very soft edge. If your mop brush gets too wet, rinse it out and dry it well with a paper towel before you resume.

5 | If you need to intensify the shadows, wait until the first layer of Liquid Shadow is completely dry. Then reapply where needed.

6 | Reposition your transparent pattern (line up the registration marks) and trace the design onto the plate. Notice the dot in the center. This is where you will place the point of your compass to draw the circles in your pattern.

Before proceeding with step 7, you will need to mix up three separate shades of a Delft Blue mixture. Keep these separated on your palette.

Delft Blue Light
Prussian Blue, Red Violet, and Titanium White (2:1:4)

Delft Blue Medium
Prussian Blue, Red Violet, and Titanium White (2:1:2)

Delft Blue Dark
Prussian Blue, Red Violet, and Titanium White (2:1:1)

PLATE

133

7 | Thin the Delft Blue Light mixture with water to create a wash. Keep the wash thin enough to still see your pattern through it, but not so thin that it is runny. Use your ¾-inch (19mm) flat and paint the outer band of the plate as shown. The brushstrokes will show but that is fine.

8 | Using your no. 1 round loaded with Delft Blue Medium, paint in the leaves, small flowers, wheat husks and shading in the middle of the plate. Also add the shading lines on the flowers.

9 | Switch to Delft Blue Dark and use your no. 1 liner to outline the flowers and leaves and to intensify some of the medium-blue center lines in the flowers.

Add some tiny lines with the Delft Blue Dark right where the flowers overlap the leaves; this creates a shadow on the leaves.

10 | Use your no. 3 round and Delft Blue Dark to paint the inside band on the plate. Do exactly the same for the outside band. Be sure to leave the outside edge white.

11 | Use your no. 8 flat or ¼-inch (6mm) flat to add the little checks around the edge. To do this, place your brush on the outside edge and pull in to the band. Make these ¼ inch (0.6cm) apart using one single stroke. When you are at the bottom, make the strokes a tiny bit shorter. This will give an appearance that the plate is sitting in the shelf's groove.

To create flawless checks I recommend using a new flat shader with a sharp chisel edge.

FLOWERS AND LAUREL TRIM

12 Using your no. 2 round, fill in the flowers in the outer band with Titanium White. While these are drying, use your no. 3 round to paint in the white laurel trim around the edges. This is painted using straight comma strokes. Still using your no. 3 round and Delft Blue Dark, begin painting in the dark laurel trim.

13 Still using Delft Blue Dark, use your no. 1 liner to outline the flowers. Completely fill in the little leaves around the five-petal flowers. For the leaves on the other flowers, use your no. 1 liner and simply outline them.

14 Fill in the flowers in the outer band with Titanium White using your no. 2 round. While these are drying, use your no. 3 round to paint in the white laurel trim around the edges. This is painted using straight comma strokes. Still using your no. 3 round and Delft Blue Dark, begin painting in the dark laurel trim.

15 Add light reflection to the plate using Titanium White and your no. 2 script liner. You may have to go over the highlights twice so the blue doesn't show through.

Using your Liquid Shadow mixture diluted with water and your no. 8 brush, add a faint shadow along the inside rim on the right side of the plate. Use the chisel edge of the same brush and shade a small line of shadow around the left side and the lower edge of the plate.

16 Replace the pattern and trace the outside of the bottle and the stems only. Using your ½-inch (12mm) flat, float Neutral Grey with water around the outside of the bottle. This does not have to be a smooth float. Use Burnt Umber and loosely sketch in the stems using your no. 2 round brush.

17 Using your 10/0 round, add a little bit of Titanium White on the right side of the stems and blend this with a little bit of Burnt Umber for the highlight.

This was an old bitters bottle, and it was very thick. Use your no. 1 liner to define the inside surface (thickness) of the bottle. Thin, light lines of Neutral Grey are what I use to define the thickness. Also define the outside edge at this time. Just paint over the edge of the lemon so your lines will flow better. Define the top (lip) of the bottle also.

Switch to your ½-inch (12mm) flat and float Neutral Grey at the top of the lip and underneath it. Wash a streak across the shoulder of the bottle as shown.

18 Using your no. 2 round with Titanium White, add highlights to the top of the rim on each side of the opening and down each side of the bottle. Around the neck add a fine line of Titanium White going across to suggest a water line.

19 Use your no. 1 script liner and the Delft Blue Dark mixture to add small lines of blue on the right side of the bottle. Also add a little bit to the left inner surface of the glass. Touch in a couple of brighter Titanium White highlights where needed. (Either add a few sparkles of light here and there or intensify the Titanium White highlights you already have.)

20 Use your no. 3 round with Burnt Umber to paint in the forsythia stems. You will highlight and shade the stems after painting the blossoms.

21 Use your no. 2 round and True Ochre to paint in a few dark background petals.

22 The next step is undercoating the lighter petals with Titanium White still using your no. 2 round. All of these petals will be painted yellow. Yellow is very translucent; this is why you need to apply the white first. When dry, apply Yellow Light to the white petals.

23 Use your no. 2 round to randomly apply Hot Shots Scorching Yellow on the right side of some of the blossoms. Use Avocado mixed with a touch of Yellow Light and paint in the calyx between the stem and the blossoms. With the same mix and brush, paint in a few small leaves here and there. These are slightly smaller than the flower petals.

24 Mix True Ochre, Burnt Umber and a touch of Titanium White (2:1:1) and use your no. 2 round to highlight the right sides of the stems. Now take just a little bit of Soft Black with enough Burnt Umber to darken it a little then shade the stems underneath any petals that overlap the stems.

25 For final highlights on the stems, mix more Titanium White into the first highlight (see step 24) color to get a really light sand color. Just intensify some of the highlighted areas on the exposed stems. Create a blossom shadow on the plate by applying some Liquid Shadow with your no. 6 mop brush to the right side of the blossoms. Switch to your no. 1 liner and paint small streaks of Titanium White highlights on a few of the blossoms.

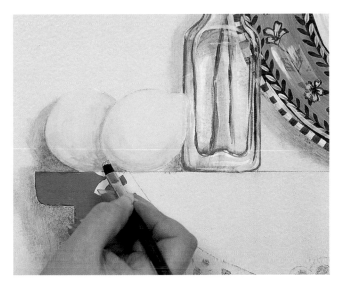

26 | Undercoat the lemons with Titanium White using your ½-inch (12mm) flat. Now basecoat the lemons with Lemon Yellow. You will need two coats of the Lemon Yellow. While the first coat is drying, use your no. 1 liner to apply a small line of Lemon Yellow to the bottom left corner of the bottle to show a reflection of color from the lemons. Once dry, use your ¼-inch (6mm) flat and Lemon Yellow and Yellow Ochre (1:1) to contour the lemons.

27 | Apply thinned True Ochre to intensify the shadow between the lemons.

28 | Use Hauser Light Green on your ½-inch (12mm) flat; apply this in a wet-on-wet manner to the left side of the rear lemon. Keep blending until you achieve the results that you desire. Also apply this lightly to the top of this lemon and to the top only on the rear lemon.

Mix Burnt Umber and True Ochre to get a dark ochre color and using the same brush, apply this to the area between the lemons to achieve a darker shadow. Apply this thinly to the bottom of the front lemon.

If at any time you aren't satisfied with how the lemons are looking, you can apply Lemon Yellow to the lemons and because it is translucent, you may find this will smooth out any imperfections.

Undercoating with white lets the top color show up in its truest form—and not be tinted by the wall color underneath. (Always undercoat a color that is translucent.)

LEMONS, *continued*

29 On the left side of the rear lemon draw a thin line of Lemon Yellow highlighting with your no. 1 liner.

30 With your ¼-inch (6mm) flat, dab on Titanium White and damp blend only the edges.

31 Paint in the blossom end of the lemon with your no. 1 liner and a mix of True Ochre and Burnt Umber (you want a light brown color). Shade it on the left side with Burnt Umber. Highlight with a couple of dots of Hauser Light Green. Paint the little wrinkles at the end with Hauser Light Green and a touch of Lemon Yellow.

Dot in the end with Burnt Umber. Apply a little Liquid Shadow with your ¼-inch flat to deepen the area where the lemons meet the shelf. With your no. 1 liner, define the lemon edge in front of the bottle with thinned Hauser Light Green.

32 Draw the bottom edge of your shelf using your ruler. Don't draw the line across the doily.

33 To accentuate the edges of the shelf, use your ½-inch (12mm) flat and float Arbor Green and Titanium White (1:1) along the top and bottom edges of your shelf.

34 Use your 1-inch (25mm) flat and float Soft Black under the shelf edge; pull this over onto the lace eyelets so the area behind the lace receives shadowing.

35 Use a water-moistened Q-tip to remove the black from the lace.

36 Use Burnt Umber and your no. 1 liner and go over the shelf edges with an irregular line in random spots to make this look like worn-off wood.

37 Use your small scruffy brush to apply your Liquid Shadow to accentuate where the lace edging hangs down in front of the shelf area. With your no. 2 round, paint in the shadow inside of the lace eyelet. This shading is important, as it adds depth to the shelf and creates the trompe l'oeil illusion of the lace hanging over the shelf.

38 Undercoat the doily with Buttermilk using your ½-inch (12mm) flat brush. Also take your no. 2 liner and carefully cover up the pattern line on the top edge of the doily.

39 Use your no. 2 round brush and Buttermilk to paint in the lace edge of the doily. Allow the coat to dry thoroughly. Apply Titanium White over the Buttermilk using your ½-inch (12mm) flat for the doily and your no. 3 round for the lace. This is not a real heavy coat of paint. It is better if some Buttermilk shows through, then the doily won't look so flat.

40 With your no. 1 round and Desert Sand, shade in and around the lace eyelet openings. Remember, in this project the light is coming from the upper right, so the eyelets should be shaded on that side. Use a very thin line for this.

41 With your no. 1 liner and Titanium White, paint the intricate stitching inside of each eyelet. This is done simply by cross-hatching.

42 Once the doily is thoroughly dry, replace the pattern and trace the small forsythia branch onto the shelf. Refer to steps 20 through 25 and repeat the same colors for this branch and blossoms as in the original forsythia branch and blossoms.

To give a bit of protection and to intensify the colors, spray your trompe l'oeil shelf with a thin coat of polyurethane. Don't forget to sign your masterpiece!

RESOURCES

Ben Franklin Craft Stores
(800)-992-9307
www.benfranklinstores.com

DecoArt, Inc
Box 327
Stanford, KY 40484
Tel: (800)-367-3047
www.decoart.com

Loew-Cornell, Inc.
563 Chestnut Ave.
Teaneck, NJ 07666-2491 USA
E-mail: sales@loew-cornell.com
Fax: (201)-836-8110
Tel: (201)-836-7070

Lowe's Companies, Inc.
P.O. Box 1111
North Wilkesboro, NC 28656
(800)-44LOWES
www.lowes.com

Saral Paper Corp.
400 East 55th Street
Suite 14C
New York, NY 10022
Tel: (212)-223-3322
Fax (212)-223-8111
E-mail: info@saralpaper.com

Scotch Brand Tape
3M Corporation
Tel: (888)-3M HELPS
(1-(888)-364-3577)

Walnut Hollow, Inc.
1409 State Road 23
Dodgeville, WI 53533
Tel: (800)-950-5101

RETAILERS IN CANADA

Crafts Canada
2745 Twenty-ninth St. NE
Calgary, Alberta T1Y 7B5

Folk Art Enterprises
P.O. Box 1088
Ridgetown, Ontario N0P 2C0
Phone: (888) 214-0062

MacPherson Craft Wholesale
83 Queen St. E.
P.O. Box 1870
St. Mary's, Ontario N4X 1C2
Phone: (519) 284-1741

Maureen McNaughton Enterprises
RR #2
Belwood, Ontario N0B 1J0
Phone: (519) 843-5648

Mercury Art & Craft Supershop
332 Wellington St.
London, Ontario N6C 4P7
Phone: (519) 434-1636

Town & Country Folk Art Supplies
93 Green Lane
Thornhill, Ontario L3T 6K6
Phone: (905) 882-0199

RETAILERS IN UNITED KINGDOM

Art Express
Index House
70 Burley Road
Leeds LS3 1JX
Tel: 0800 731 4185
www.artexpress.co.uk

Crafts World (head office only)
No 8 North Street, Guildford
Surrey GU1 4AF
Tel: 07000 757070
Telephone for local store

Chroma Colour Products
Unit 5 Pilton Estate
Pitlake
Croydon CR0 3RA
Tel: 020 8688 1991
www.chromacolour.com

Green & Stone
259 King's Road
London SW3 5EL
Tel: 020 7352 0837
greenandstone@enterprise.net

Hobbycrafts (head office only)
River Court
Southern Sector
Bournemouth International
Airport
Christchurch
Dorset BH23 6SE
Tel: 0800 272387 freephone
Telephone for local store

Homecrafts Direct
P.O. Box 38
Leicester LE1 9BU
Tel: 0116 251 3139
Mail order service

INDEX

WATCH FOR THESE OTHER EXCITING TITLES FROM NORTH LIGHT BOOKS!

Learn how to create stunning illusions on walls, floors, and ceilings. Here's all the instruction you need to use inexpensive, laser-cut plastic stencils with skill and confidence. Author Melanie Royals shows you how to combine stencils, shields, and tape with simple paint techniques, buy the proper equipment, prepare surfaces, manipulate stencils, and apply paint. The final section provides more advanced instruction for large-scale projects.

ISBN 1-58180-028-2, paperback, 128 pages, #31668-K

Handpainting furniture is fun, inexpensive, and—with this book—easy to do. You'll find nine step-by-step projects inside, plus an exciting array of realistic scenes and trompe l'oeil effects for decorating all kinds of furniture. Clear instructions leave nothing to chance and cover everything from preparing surfaces and scaling up drawings to techniques for giving each piece an authentic, antique look.

ISBN 0-89134-980-4, paperback, 128 pages, #31539-K

Take your decorative painting to an exciting new level of depth and dimension by creating the illusion of reality—one that transforms your work from good to extraordinary! Patti DeRenzo, CDA, shows you how to master the building blocks of realism—value, temperature, intensity and form—to render three-dimensional images with height, depth and width.

ISBN 0-89134-995-2, paperback, 128 pages, #31661-K

This book is the must-have one-stop reference for decorative painters, crafters, home decorators and do-it-yourselfers. It's packed with solutions to every painting challenge, including surface preparation, lettering, borders, faux finishes, strokework techniques and more! You'll also find five fun-to-paint projects designed to instruct, challenge and entertain you—no matter what your skill level.

ISBN 1-58180-062-2, paperback, 256 pages, #31803-K

These books and other fine North Light titles are available from your local art & craft retailer, bookstore, online supplier or by calling 1-800-221-5831.